Why Don't We Defend Better?

Data Breaches, Risk Management, and Public Policy

T0187522

Why Don't We Defend Better?

Data Breaches, Risk Management, and Public Policy

Robert H. Sloan
Richard Warner

CRC Press
Taylor & Francis Group
Boca Raton London New York

CRC Press is an imprint of the
Taylor & Francis Group, an **informa** business

CRC Press
Taylor & Francis Group
6000 Broken Sound Parkway NW, Suite 300
Boca Raton, FL 33487-2742

First issued in paperback 2020

ISBN-13: 978-0-8153-5662-2 (hbk)
ISBN-13: 978-0-367-78791-2 (pbk)

Library of Congress Cataloging-in-Publication Data

Names: Sloan, Robert H., author. | Warner, Richard, 1946- author.
Title: Why don't we defend better? : data breaches, risk management, and public policy / Robert H. Sloan, Richard Warner.
Description: First edition. | Boca Raton, FL : CRC Press/Taylor & Francis Group, [2019]
Identifiers: LCCN 2019010377| ISBN 9780815356622 (hardback : acid-free paper) | ISBN 9781351127301 (ebook)
Subjects: LCSH: Computer networks--Security measures--Government policy. | Computer security--Government policy. | Business--Data processing--Security measures. | Computer crimes--Risk assessment.
Classification: LCC TK5105.59 .S585 2019 | DDC 005.8--dc23
LC record available at https://lccn.loc.gov/2019010377

Visit the Taylor & Francis Web site at
http://www.taylorandfrancis.com

and the CRC Press Web site at
http://www.crcpress.com

Contents

Authors

Robert H. Sloan is a Professor and Head of the Department of Computer Science at the University of Illinois at Chicago (UIC). He has a BS in mathematics from Yale, and an SM and PhD in computer science from the Massachusetts Institute of Technology (MIT). He is a member of the U.S. Department of Homeland Security Privacy and Integrity Advisory Committee. In the early 2000s, he served as a Program Director at the National Science Foundation. In recent years, he has overseen the growth of the UIC Computer Science Department from 28 to 55 faculty (and growing). Dr. Sloan's current scholarly work includes public policy issues in computer security and privacy as well as computer science education. In the past, he also worked in theoretical computer science and artificial intelligence. He has published over 100 articles, as well as a book he coauthored with Richard Warner, *Unauthorized Access: The Crisis in Online Privacy and Information Security* (Chapman & Hall/CRC Press, 2013).

Richard Warner is a Professor Norman and Edna Freehling Scholar, Chicago–Kent College of Law. He has a BA in English literature, Stanford University; PhD (philosophy), University of California, Berkeley; JD, University of Southern California, Los Angeles. He is the Faculty Director of Chicago–Kent's Center for Law and Computers, the Cofounder and Director of the School of American Law, the Codirector of the Center for National Security and Human Rights, and the Head of the School of American Law, a Chicago–Kent affiliated program with several international branches. He is a member of the U.S. Secret Service's Electronic and Financial Crimes Taskforce. His research interests include privacy, the regulation of machine learning, and philosophical theories of communication. He has published extensively in the legal and philosophical literature. His most recent book, coauthored with Robert J. Sloan, is *Unauthorized Access: The Crisis in Online Privacy and Information Security* (Chapman & Hall/CRC Press, 2013).

CHAPTER 1

Introduction

V ERY CONSERVATIVELY ESTIMATED, THERE are more than three data breaches a day[1] with a high aggregate cost. One recent study puts the average cost per business of a breach at $3.86 million.[2] Such estimates are controversial,[3] but it is clear that breaches impose significant losses on society. Security experts have long explained how to better defend against hackers. Why don't we defend better? Why instead does society tolerate a significant loss that it has the means to avoid? There is more than one reason, but we focus on what we will argue is the most important one: the lack of sufficient information about the cost of breaches and about the probability of their occurrence. That lack of information can cause organizations to spend the wrong amount on defending themselves against breaches, typically underspending.

Our focus may surprise some. Why concentrate on *defense*? Isn't a good offense an important part of the solution? Why not propose better ways for law enforcement to identify and shut down hackers? It would of course be foolish to deny law enforcement an important role, but it is far from a complete solution. There will always be some people who will engage in illegal behavior as long as they see a positive risk-reward calculation, and a significant number of people will see a positive reward since it can be hard to locate and prosecute hackers, especially in foreign jurisdictions.

Law enforcement is in the business of locating and shutting down hackers, not in preventing them from being able to hack in the first place. Law enforcement will always make decisions about where to spend their limited resources based partially on the likelihood that they can attribute a breach to a particular criminal or group of criminals, and then locate and successfully prosecute those criminals. Each attribution, location, and prosecution can be quite difficult. So defenses are critical. Defenses benefit the defender by reducing losses, and they benefit law enforcement by reducing the amount of successful hacking it needs to investigate.

We begin by explaining what we mean by a data breach.

WHAT IS A DATA BREACH?

We characterize data breaches by using the traditional division of information security into confidentiality, integrity, and availability—sometimes referred to as CIA, or as the CIA triad. *Confidentiality* consists of keeping information away from those not authorized to possess it. We expect confidentiality for telephone conversations, financial transactions, and medical records. *Integrity* consists of preventing information from being altered by those not authorized to alter it. We need integrity for financial instruments, and both integrity and confidentiality for texts and emails. *Availability* consists of making computer systems available to authorized users. It's easy to maintain the confidentiality and integrity of information if you don't need availability. Simply put the information on one computer and permanently turn off that computer, or put it in a bank vault and leave it there.

From the point of view of the organizations breached and the consumers affected, data breaches are primarily a matter of confidentiality. In many breaches, hackers obtain credit card data that should have remained confidential. Examples include the Wyndham Hotel, Target, and Equifax breaches (which we discuss below), as well as the Home Depot, Macy's, and Sears breaches of 2018, and many others. In addition, in many breaches, including the Wyndham Hotel, Target, and Equifax, as well as the Anthem and U.S. Office of Personnel Management breaches, other personal information, such as Social Security numbers, emails, and phone numbers that should have stayed confidential, was breached.

From the point of view of the information security defenders, there are also massive integrity violations at play. Software that should not have been allowed to run on a computer ran, violating the integrity of those computer systems. We return to the integrity prong of the CIA triad when we discuss the Internet of Things (IoT) in Chapter 5. Compromised integrity on the IoT can have serious consequences—car accidents, malfunctioning medical devices, failing power grids, and so on.

A narrow use of the label "data breach" restricts it to breaches of confidentiality along with the compromised integrity they involve. When data breaches in this sense involve unauthorized access to sensitive information, they constitute invasions of privacy. A broader use applies the label to events that corrupt, destroy, or block access to information. Data breaches then include denial of service attacks, ransomware attacks, and destructive hacking that corrupts or destroys data. These are not instances of unauthorized possession or viewing of data, but they do interfere with data in ways that can be highly disruptive. The table summarizes the typology.

	Data Taken/ Viewed	Site Access Denied	Data Hidden	Data Corrupted/ Destroyed
Confidentiality	Data breach			
Integrity	Data breach[a]	Denial of service	Ransomware	Destructive hacking
Availability		Denial of service	Ransomware	Destructive hacking

[a] As a part of the breach of confidentiality.

We focus primarily on data breaches in the narrow "data taken/ viewed" sense until we turn to the IoT in Chapter 5, where we consider the "data hidden" ransomware cases and the breaches of integrity involved in destructive hacking.

FOUR EXAMPLES

Before we go any further, let's take a look at four among the thousands of significant data breaches in the past 15 years or so. For many data breaches, only a limited amount of information is publicly available. For our first two breaches, however, a fair amount is known, which is one reason we are discussing them. The late 2013 Target breach received a great deal of coverage by the news media and was also the subject of a detailed report by the U.S. Senate Committee on Commerce, Science, and Transportation. The Wyndham Hotels breach, or rather, the series of three breaches of Wyndham hotels between 2008 and late 2009, was the subject of legal action by the U.S. Federal Trade Commission (FTC), creating a public record. We will also discuss two more recent breaches where less is publicly known: Equifax, the biggest breach of 2017, and Marriott, the biggest breach of 2018.

Target

On December 19, 2013, Americans learned that Target stores had suffered a massive breach and that tens of millions of credit card numbers had been stolen. This was headline news, and it eventually became clear that about 40 million Target customers had credit card information stolen, and another 70 million had other personal information, such as addresses and phone numbers, stolen.[4] In the fullness of time, Target's CIO and CEO would both lose their jobs,[5] banks would reissue about 21 million credit cards to vast numbers of Americans (including one of the authors of this monograph) at a cost of about $200 million,[6] and Target's expenses would total $291 million.[7]

How could such a thing happen? What went wrong? The short answer is, *many* things went wrong. A fairly common pattern in disasters in both real life and fiction is that several different things go wrong, and the sum total of those occurrences causes the disaster. This is the story of the Target breach. The breach was very well-documented by the mainstream media, several excellent summary reports, and excellent original journalism by Brian Krebbs, who specializes in computer security reporting on his Krebbs on Security blog. Most of what we describe comes from one of these sources. However, a bit of what we write is necessarily speculative, since Target did not disclose more than they had to.

All the stolen credit cards were used at Target during the prime Christmas shopping season, between November 27 and December 18, 2013.[8] However, the story starts many months earlier. The beginning might indicate that it should have a happy ending. Six months before the breach, Target began installing a $1.6 million malware defense system from the well-regarded company FireEye, including a team that was monitoring the system in Bangalore, India.[9]

Meanwhile, sometime many months before the attack, the hackers may well have researched Target's overall electronic layout and defenses—using a plain old Google search. Some of this information was available on the web, including lists of Target contractors.[10] At least two months before credit card numbers started to be stolen, the hackers broke into Fazio Mechanical Services, a small HVAC contractor that worked for Target. The hackers started by sending a phishing email. The phish was successful: Some Fazio employee clicked where they shouldn't have clicked. Moreover, Fazio was running only a free consumer version of anti-malware software that did not regularly update its list of malware signatures to defend against. The phish succeeded in installing malware at Fazio. The malware stole Fazio's username and password for logging on to Target's portal for its contractors.

Hackers gaining access to Target's contractor portal should not have been a big deal. A basic principle of good computer security is that the most sensitive parts of the systems (such as cash registers) should be isolated from other parts that are open to many people (such as vendor and contractor portals). Nevertheless, the hackers were able to move from Target's contractor portal to the heart of

Target's systems. In late November 2013, the hackers installed two different sets of malware. The first was malware that actually stole the credit card numbers from Target's point of sale (POS) systems (i.e., their cash registers); the second, was malware that exfiltrated the stolen information back to servers controlled by the hackers, at least one of which was located in Russia.[11]

All companies that accept credit cards must adhere to and pass audits for adherence to the Payment Card Industry (PCI) Data Security Standard (DSS). Of course, a large retail company like Target was PCI compliant, and had passed a PCI audit in September 2013. The PCI standards then and now require encryption of credit card data, and properly encrypted credit card numbers have no value to thieves. However, the 2013 PCI version only required that credit card numbers be encrypted before they *leave* a POS system. The malware that was installed scraped the memory of Target's POS terminals, and the credit card numbers in Target's POS terminals were unencrypted from card swipe time being transmitted out of the POS terminal for verification. This scraping issue was something that security experts were aware of in 2013, but the PCI standard did not force encryption at the time of swipe until a later version.

However, all was not lost for Target. The FireEye alert system "worked beautifully,"[12] and Target received one set of alarms on November 30 and more on December 2, when the hackers evidently updated the malware that they had installed.[13] Unfortunately, Target ignored the alerts from FireEye. It is not known (except to a few Target employees and former employees) *why* Target ignored the alerts. It could well be that Target's staff was incompetent or badly trained. It might also be that the FireEye system sent frequent alarms about common minor probe events, and that Target's staff inevitably came to ignore them. Massive over-alerting is a fairly common problem with intrusion detection systems.

In any event, Target officials would eventually testify before Congress that they were unaware of the breach until the Department of Justice notified them on December 12, 2013.

This breach had a large number of but-for causes. Several were serious flaws in Target's security. Target should have had proper security that would not allow hackers to go from the contractors' portal to its most vital systems. Target should have detected and *reacted to* the malware that was installed on its POS terminals. Indeed, It should never have allowed malware to be installed into their POS system in the first place. The POS terminal should not have been treated like a laptop computer where one could install any software. It should have had a *whitelist*, a short list of programs that were the only software allowed to run on it. A POS terminal is an obvious point of vulnerability.

The FireEye system Target used reportedly had a setting to automatically disable suspected malware, and Target might have employed it, although that approach also has its risks. If FireEye made a mistake, they could have accidentally shut down Target's POS systems.

Fazio Mechanical Systems should have trained its employees to avoid phishing, and should have purchased small-business caliber anti-malware software for its own computers, which would have detected the malware used to steal Fazio's credentials. Some analysts have written that Target should have had computer security standards for all its vendors, but that might have been unrealistic, especially in 2013, when there was not quite as much concern about the computer breach epidemic as there was after the Target breach.

Target might have sought to make its POS system as safe as possible, and encrypted credit cards at swipe time, rather than simply meeting the PCI standard. Then again, retail has a low profit margin, and the whole point of standards like PCI is that companies can rely on the standard. The PCI standards themselves probably should have required encryption at credit card swipe time by 2013, but the PCI organization is pressured to keep the costs of compliance down.

So, as we said, there were many places where this breach might have been stopped but wasn't. Next, we consider the question of how big a loss Target took. Analysts have split opinions. One answer is, "Target lost $291 million, an awful lot of money."

However, insurance payments to Target brought the net loss down to $201 million,[14] and those losses were tax deductible, so the after-tax loss was no more than $145 million.[15] Target's 2014 gross income from sales net of the cost of the goods it sold was about $19 billion.[16] In other words, Target's after-tax loss from the breach was a bit *under one-tenth of 1% of its 2014 income*, so maybe the breach wasn't such a big loss, at least not to the Target corporation. But others lost plenty. Banks spent about $200 million replacing credit cards, and eventually recovered only $39 million of that cost from Target. Tens of millions of consumers had the nuisance of getting replacement credit cards, and some unknown number were victims of identity theft of various sorts stemming from the breach.

Wyndham Hotels

Wyndham Hotels is a worldwide hotel corporation. In 2008–2009, its network security was quite weak. It had no firewalls at all, did not encrypt stored credit card numbers, failed to patch software on a regular basis, left original factory setting passwords unchanged, failed to appropriately limit third-party vendor access (by restricting connections to specific IP addresses and granting only temporary and limited access), and failed to adequately monitor its network for unauthorized access.[17] In 2008 and 2009, hackers breached the network three times and stole personal and payment card information from more than 600,000 accounts resulting in $10.6 million in fraudulent charges.[18] The breach also cost Wyndham millions in litigation.[19] Incidentally, hotel breaches continue to be a problem: There have been at least 25 hotel data breaches in the years 2014 through 2018, including at Marriott, which we will discuss, as well as at Radisson, Hilton, Hyatt, and the Trump Hotel Collection.[20]

In the first Wyndham breach in 2008, hackers broke into the local network of a hotel in Phoenix, Arizona. The local hotel had access to Wyndham's network through its hotel property management system, which allowed local hotels to handle activities such as booking, pricing, and marketing through Wyndham's network. Wyndham had no firewalls, nor any other means to adequately limit access between local hotels and the Wyndham network. Using a brute-force password guesser, the hackers gained access to an administrator account on Wyndham's network. This gave them access to unencrypted information for over 500,000 accounts, which they sent to a domain in Russia.

Even after this attack, Wyndham failed to monitor its network for the presence of the malware used. The second breach occurred in March 2009, when hackers gained access to Wyndham's network through an administrator's account in a Wyndham data center. Since Wyndham failed to monitor its network for the malware used in the previous attack, the hackers were able to install the same malware as in the 2008 attack. Even after that second attack, Wyndham failed to adequately limit and monitor access through its property management systems, and they were hacked again in 2009, through another administrator account on a local hotel network.

The FTC investigated the data breaches and found that Wyndham's security procedures unreasonably exposed consumers to the risk of losses from unauthorized access to their data. Wyndham responded with a court case that challenged the FTC's authority to regulate the hotel's security procedures. The Federal Appellate Court upheld the FTC's regulatory authority and held that Wyndham had fair notice of the relevant standard of reasonableness. Wyndham should have realized that, in determining how much to invest in security, "the relevant inquiry ... is a cost-benefit analysis that considers a number of relevant factors, including the probability and expected size of reasonably unavoidable harms to consumers given a certain level of cybersecurity and the costs to consumers that would arise from investment in stronger cybersecurity."[21]

Equifax

The Equifax data breach was the largest and most publicized data breach of 2017 with good reason. This incident affected 148 million Americans—56% of adult Americans. Almost all of them, about 145.5 million, had their names, date of birth, *and* Social Security numbers compromised.[22] The breach was really entirely Equifax's fault. As we will discuss, it is unclear whether Equifax or its top executives suffered any meaningful long-term negative aftereffects from the breach.

Equifax, if it was known to consumers at all before this breach, was known as one of the handful of major credit bureaus. Beyond that, Equifax is also a major data broker. Even though the data broker role is much less well known to the general public, it is important. Equifax and other data brokers collect, analyze, and then sell data about all consumers. (The threats to privacy posed by data brokers, beyond the threat of their being breached, are outside the scope of this book, but we and many others in the privacy community have written extensively elsewhere about data brokers' threat to privacy.[23]) In both its capacities, Equifax holds massive amounts of data about almost all U.S. consumers.

Unlike the Target breach, where there were a host of security problems, the Equifax breach had only one main problem, and one ancillary factor. The main reason the breach occurred is that Equifax did not patch vulnerable software that it was repeatedly told was vulnerable.

Equifax used open-source software called Apache Struts from the Apache Software Foundation for its website. In February 2017, the Apache Software Foundation was notified of a serious vulnerability in Apache Struts, and they issued a public announcement of this vulnerability as well as a patch on March 7, 2017. In addition to the public announcement from the Apache Foundation, one day later on March 8, the Department of Homeland Security's U.S. Computer Emergency Readiness Team (US-CERT) sent Equifax a notification that they needed to patch

Apache Struts. By March 9, the computer press was reporting that the Apache Struts vulnerability was being widely exploited.[24] Nevertheless, Equifax did not fully patch Apache Struts on all its systems *until late July.* In May, hackers began exploiting the Apache Struts vulnerability to steal the 148 million records from Equifax.

Needless to say, $10 billion plus market cap companies holding large amounts of consumer data, such as Equifax, that receive a notice from DHS that some software needs to be patched immediately should not delay the patching for four months. There is no excuse for this failure to patch.

There is, however, an explanation for why hackers were able to exfiltrate millions of records starting in May without Equifax noticing it until late July. The device Equifax was using to monitor the security of the system that the data was stolen from was inactive for *19 months* because of an expired security certificate. It is not publicly known why Equifax failed to keep its security certificates up to date. Equifax finally updated that certificate on July 29, 2017, and immediately noticed the suspicious web traffic. It took the attacked system offline on July 30, ending the cyberattack. Equifax received more negative publicity for not notifying the public of this massive data breach until September 7, and generally handling breach public relations (PR) and public remediation efforts badly.

Did the breach seriously harm Equifax or its CEO? As with the Target breach, the answer is unclear. Several top executives, including CEO Richard Smith, were forced to resign. Smith lost his 2017 $3 million bonus, but was allowed to resign with a remarkable $90 million golden parachute.[25] Equifax's stock price did plunge from $142 a share to $92 a share in the immediate aftermath of the public disclosure of the breach in September 2017, but the stock had recovered to $138 a share by mid-September 2018. As of mid-April 2018, Equifax reported that they had spent $243 million on the breach, of which $50 million had been covered by insurance.[26] The net cost of $193 million represents about 0.6% of Equifax's annual $3 billion in revenue.

Marriott

In late November 2018, as this book was being completed, the public learned of an even larger data breach than Equifax. The Marriott International chain had *383 million* consumer records stolen,[27] one of the largest number of records ever stolen (though definitely behind the Yahoo breach of 2013). In many cases, it appears that passport data was taken. The records of guests who used the Starwood reservation system between 2014 and September 2018, including Sheraton and Westin Hotels among other properties, were stolen. (Marriott bought the Starwood Group in 2016.) As of this writing, there continues to be a lack of good public information about *how* the breach occurred and how it went undetected for four years. We can sensibly speculate that something was very wrong with Marriott's defenses, because such a large data theft went undetected for four years.

Initial reports suggest that the data was stolen by Chinese hackers working for the Chinese government.[28] Hacking by nation-states has definitely occurred in recent years. China is known to have been responsible for the 2014 U.S. Office of Personnel Management (OPM) breach and the 2014 Anthem breach.[29] Personal information on North Korean defectors to South Korea was lost in a data breach of the South Korean government agency that resettles the defectors.[30] It's not yet known who was responsible for that breach, but the North Korean government is the obvious suspect. Nation-states have also carried out other kinds of cyberattacks on organizations, rather than simply stealing data. The United States and Israel, working together in 2009, created the Stuxnet virus to sabotage centrifuges being used by the Iranian government to develop nuclear weapons grade uranium.[31] Russia has attacked power grids in the Ukraine, and Iran attacked a casino in Las Vegas.[32]

Nation-state breaches raise some issues that are beyond the scope of this work. One is the problem of attribution, figuring out who the identity of the attacker. This can be quite problematic for any data breach, and especially if the attackers have the technical resources available to a nation-state and are trying to confuse the attribution. Another issue is how such attacks can be controlled by treaties or international law, including the law of war. A third issue is whether it is economically sensible for a company to defend against the sort of concerted targeted attack using massive resources that only nation-states have.

These issues are largely beyond the scope of this book. However, the third issue may *not* arise too often in practice. While the government of China (or Russia, or the United States, for that matter) certainly *can* use overwhelming resources to attack extremely well-defended sites that may not often happen in practice. Given the choice, even nation-states will prefer to attack poorly defended organizations. Consider China's breaches of Anthem and OPM: Anthem had a fundamental problem with lack of encryption,[33] and in 2014, OPM's data was "loosely guarded."[34] Starwood and Marriott's failure to even *detect* the breach for four years hints that their security was weak as well, though as of this writing it is too soon to say.

Now that we have seen a few examples, let's turn to the topic of why security against breaches is so often weak.

WHY DON'T WE DEFEND BETTER?

Would you throw money into an incinerator or use it in productive ways? So, why does society throw billions into the incinerator of data breaches?

We focus on two types of losses—business losses (lost sales, theft of intellectual property, regulatory fines, and so on) and consumer losses from unauthorized access to information held by businesses (identity theft, credit card fraud, a sense of invaded privacy, and so on). With regard to both types of loss, society as a whole would be best off if businesses adequately approximated the following *risk management goal*. Choose defensive measures to minimize the following sum: the cost of the defensive measures and all the expected losses with those defensive measures. Spending significantly less or more on defense wastes money. As one security expert put it, "enterprises find it incredibly difficult to demonstrate active control over their cyber hygiene."[35]

The first step in understanding how to remedy this situation is to distinguish between two versions of the risk management goal. The *business* risk management goal is to minimize the sum of the cost of the defensive measures and all the expected *business* losses with those defensive measures. The *consumer* risk management goal is to minimize the sum of the cost of the defensive measures and all the expected business *and consumer* losses with those defensive measures.

Businesses fail to adequately approximate the consumer risk management goal. This is not surprising. Profit-driven businesses ignore consumer losses unless those losses also impose significant losses on the business.[36] What is puzzling is that businesses fail to adequately approximate the *business* risk management goal. After all, the long-run net profit maximizing approach for a business is to adequately approximate the risk management goal *at least with regard to its business losses*. So, why do businesses fall short of this goal? Part of the explanation is that corporate culture has struggled—and still struggles—with the risk management necessary for effective cybersecurity.[37] While we do not minimize the importance of the corporate culture problem, we focus on a deeper problem, a problem that would remain even for a corporate leadership dedicated to pursuing the risk management goal.

THE LACK OF INFORMATION PROBLEM

A business should choose defensive measures to minimize the sum of the cost of the defensive measures and all the expected losses with those defensive measures. However, businesses lack the information needed to estimate the expected loss avoided for a given company from adopting a particular type of defense against a type of data breach. Consider the calculation:

Expected loss avoided = Expected loss without defense
— Sum of expected loss with defense and cost of defense

The cost of a defense is usually easy to know, but the other two items need to be calculated:

Expected loss without defense = Loss if type of breach occurs
  × Probability of its occurrence without defense

Expected loss with defense = Loss if type of breach occurs
  × Probability of its occurrence with defense

We do not have sufficiently accurate estimates of either the likely loss from a type of breach or the probability of a breach occurring either with or without a particular type of defense. A World Economic Forum report paints an accurate, if disturbing, picture of the lack of relevant data. "Unknowns concerning the scale and impact of cyber threats, as well as relative levels of vulnerability, threatens paralysis."[38] Large organizations "struggle to structure cyber resilience decisions and investments."[39]

The report identifies two sources of uncertainty: the two that were just mentioned. The first is that the magnitude of the losses is not sufficiently well known: there are "[u]nknowns concerning the scale and impact of cyber threats." The second is that the probability of a loss is not sufficiently well known: there are "[u]nknowns concerning … relative levels of vulnerability." This puts a significant roadblock in the way of pursuing the risk management goal for business losses.

How might this uncertainty play out in practice? Consider Target's *a priori* position before the breach. Perhaps the probability of a $145 million breach over the coming five years is 1%; perhaps it is 10%. An expenditure of $100,000 a year, or $500,000 in total, might drive that five-year breach probability down to 0.5%, or down to 0.1%, or not move it at all, because $100,000 a year isn't enough. Maybe $1 million a year is required to move the five-year breach probability down to 0.5%. For many of these numbers, buying more defense meets the business risk minimization goal. For example, it would be worthwhile to spend a million dollars a year to drive the likelihood of a breach from 5% to 0.5%. (Spending $5 million for an expected savings of just over $6.5 million.) It would be worthwhile to spend $100,000 a year if that would lower the breach probability just from 1% to 0.5%. However, the actual probabilities matter. For example, it is *not* worthwhile to spend $1 million a year on added defense if that only moves the five-year breach probability from 3% to 0.5%.

Some may object that the lack of information about relevant probabilities and costs does not leave businesses helpless. They can still make reasonable decisions about information security. Lacking sufficient objective information, they can turn to subjective expert judgments and a variety of sophisticated analytic techniques that make use of them. This is a reasonable approach given the current lack of objective information. It is no surprise, then, that subjective expert judgment risk management is the approach of security outsourcing companies such as Healthguard Cyber Risk Management and FireEye.[40] This does not, however, obviate the need to do better. The ultimate goal is to approximate the risk management goal, and you cannot reliably do that without adequate objective information about probabilities and losses. Subjective judgment approaches make *educated guesses* about these probabilities and losses, and those guesses may lead a business to invest far less or far more than required to meet the risk management goal. Of course, needing to do better does not mean we can. Are there ways to better approximate the risk management goal? Yes, if we can aggregate sufficient information about the probabilities and costs of data breaches. We propose ways to do this in Chapter 4.

A preliminary step is to distinguish between three different contexts in which the lack of information problem arises. The three problems correspond to three types of vulnerabilities. Our notion of a vulnerability is a standard one: a property of a program, computer, network, or person that hackers can exploit to gain unauthorized access. Vulnerabilities come in three types (overlapping at the edges): software, security management, and human. In each case, distinguishing between these problems provides the essential background for determining how to approximate both the business and consumer risk management goals. In the case of *business* risk management, solving the lack of information problem would on its own be a major step forward in solving the lack of adequate defense against *business* losses. Businesses sufficiently concerned with long-run profitability would seek to approximate the risk management goal with regard to those losses. Approximating the *consumer* risk management goal is more problematic. One cannot solve the problem merely by supplying businesses with relevant information about probabilities and losses. Profit-driven businesses will not defend against *consumer* losses that do not also impose losses on them.

This is the well-known problem of negative externalities. A *negative externality* is a cost of an economic activity by one party that is imposed on another without any corresponding costs falling on the first party. Classic examples include the costs of air or water pollution from manufacturing and the cost of diminished efficiency of antibiotics for the whole population caused by overuse of antibiotics by particular individuals or physicians. Negative externalities typically lead not just to costs being shifted from one party to another, but to a net decrease in benefit to society as a whole. In most cases, society overall would be better off with some investment in efforts to reduce pollution, the overuse of antibiotics, or number of data breaches. However, since they do not bear the loss, a profit-driven first party will not invest any time, effort, or money in eliminating negative externalities. Such investment will just reduce profits. Thus, we need to change the incentive structure to ensure that businesses have a sufficient incentive to protect against consumer losses.

We consider how to provide that incentive in Chapters 2 through 4. Our goal is to match policies to problems, not to work out those policies in detail. Focusing on policy details can make you miss the forest for the trees. We offer a view of the forest.

Software Vulnerabilities

A software vulnerability is an unlocked door. The hacker finds it and walks in. Software programs currently contain an unacceptable number of vulnerabilities. That is not inevitable. Software engineers know how to minimize (though, alas, not how to totally eliminate) vulnerabilities.[41] How to write individual computer programs well, and the basics of software engineering are fairly well-settled subjects. As we will explain in Chapter 2, consumers are a large part of the problem. They currently reject more secure software because it is expensive, inconvenient to use, and slower to market. Instead, they demand inexpensive, easy-to-use, quick-to-market software, and so that is what software producers provide. Hence, consumer-facing software frequently contains vulnerabilities.

Security Management Vulnerabilities

Security management vulnerabilities arise from the failures of organizations to employ adequate technical defenses. Failure to adequately manage defense caused the Equifax breach, which we have seen was caused by a failure to patch in a timely manner. Fazio Mechanical in the Target breach is another example. Fazio failed to run adequate anti-malware software. We don't know exactly what vulnerability the hackers exploited at Fazio, but a reasonable guess is that the phishing email contained a PDF or Excel attachment, designed to exploit vulnerabilities in a widespread piece of consumer-facing software: either Adobe PDF reading software or Microsoft Excel.

We discuss security management vulnerabilities in Chapter 3.

Human Vulnerabilities

The main human vulnerability hackers exploit is the human propensity to trust. Vampire movies are a good analogy. In classic vampire movies, vampires can't enter a house unless invited in, so the audience cringes when some innocent, ignorant person asks the obvious-to-the-audience vampire to cross the threshold. Similarly, far too many invite hackers to cross the threshold of their computers and networks. Phishing is a good example of such an attack. Phishing is the use of electronic communication that masquerades as being from someone trustworthy in order to gain unauthorized access to information. We discuss human vulnerabilities in Chapter 7.

LEGAL REGULATION

As the lawyer Thomas Smedinghoff notes, there are information security laws that "obligate companies to establish and maintain 'reasonable' or 'appropriate' security measures, controls, safeguards, or procedures."[42] To evaluate how effective those laws currently are, think of computer scientists' knowledge of how to defend against unauthorized access as generating a "shopping list" of options, and imagine a spectrum of spending. Instances of egregious underspending occupy one end. Instances of excessive overspending, the other.

The middle is home to adequate approximation to the risk management goal. An effective reasonableness standard would mean organizations incurring FTC fines or losing civil suits in cases starting at the egregious underspending end of the spectrum and reaching significantly toward but stopping short of the adequate approximation middle.

That is not what is seen. The cases where breached organizations lose in court are all instances of egregious underspending, as in Wyndham, or a major failure to properly use defenses as in Target. The explanation is the lack of relevant information about probabilities and costs, as we argue in the following chapters.

ENDNOTES

1. "2018 Data Breaches," Identity Theft Resource Center, December 5, 2018, https://www.idtheftcenter.org/2018-data-breaches/, showing 1338 data breaches in the first 340 days of 2018. The ITRC uses a narrow definition of a breach: a data breach is "an incident in which an individual name plus a Social Security number, driver's license number, medical record or financial record (credit/debit cards included) is potentially put at risk because of exposure." In addition,

they appear to report only breaches with some connection to the United States. Other types of unauthorized access to computers and networks can "potentially put at risk because of exposure" a great deal of other sorts of sensitive information, so data breaches would be even more common on a broader understanding of a data breach.

2. Ponemon Institute, "2018 Cost of Data Breach Study: Global Overview," 2018, https://www.ibm.com/security/data-breach.
3. See, e.g., Maria Korolov, $154 or 58 Cents – What's the Real Cost of a Breached Data Record? CSO Online, 2015, http://www.csoonline.com/article/2931839/data-breach/154-or-58-cents-whats-the-real-cost-of-a-breached-data-record.html.
4. Majority Staff Report for Chairman Rockefeller, "A 'Kill Chain' Analysis of the 2013 Target Data Breach" (United States Senate Committee on Commerce, Science, and Transportation, March 6, 2014), https://www.commerce.senate.gov/public/_cache/files/24d3c229-4f2f-405d-b8db-a3a67f183883/23E30AA955B5C00FE57CFD709621592C.2014-0325-target-kill-chain-analysis.pdf.
5. T. Radichel, "Case Study: Critical Controls That Could Have Prevented Target Breach," SANS Institute InfoSec Reading Room, 2014.
6. B. Krebbs, "The Target Breach, by the Numbers," *Krebs on Security* (blog), May 14, 2014, https://krebsonsecurity.com/2014/05/the-target-breach-by-the-numbers/.
7. J. Daly, "Expenses From the Home Depot and Target Data Breaches Surpass $500 Million," *Digital Transactions*, May 26, 2016, https://www.digitaltransactions.net/expenses-from-the-home-depot-and-target-data-breaches-surpass-500-million/.
8. Majority Staff Report for Chairman Rockefeller, "A 'Kill Chain' Analysis of the 2013 Target Data Breach."
9. M. Riley et al., "Missed Alarms and 40 Million Stolen Credit Card Numbers: How Target Blew It," *Bloomberg Businessweek*, March 17, 2014, https://www.bloomberg.com/news/articles/2014-03-13/target-missed-warnings-in-epic-hack-of-credit-card-data.
10. Radichel, "Case Study: Critical Controls That Could Have Prevented Target Breach."
11. Majority Staff Report for Chairman Rockefeller, "A 'Kill Chain' Analysis of the 2013 Target Data Breach."
12. M. Riley et al., "Missed Alarms and 40 Million Stolen Credit Card Numbers."
13. M. Riley et al.

14. J. Daly, "Expenses from the Home Depot and Target Data Breaches Surpass $500 Million."
15. B. Dean et al., "Sorry Consumers, Companies Have Little Incentive to Invest in Better Cybersecurity," *Quartz* (blog), March 5, 2015, http://qz.com/356274/cybersecurity-breaches-hurt-consumers-companies-not-so-much/.
16. "Target Corp.," accessed August 7, 2018, https://www.marketwatch.com/investing/stock/tgt.
17. See C. Enloe, "Lessons to Be Learned from the Wyndham Hotels Data Breach," *Lexology* (blog), December 17, 2015, https://www.lexology.com/library/detail.aspx?g=7f31b155-04f4-4fd2-87e9-265dbca2b81d. Other significant lapses were that Wyndham had absolutely no restrictions on where people could log in from (i.e., no restrictions on any specific IP addresses) and had various passwords that were unchanged from the original factory setting.
18. A Federal Trade Commission (FTC) investigation led to *FTC v. Wyndham Worldwide Corp.*, 799 F. 3d 236 (D.C. 2015). Wyndham ultimately settled the case with the Federal Trade Commission, agreeing to maintain a comprehensive security program with annual audits by the FTC. Tracy Kitten, "Wyndham Agrees to Settle FTC Breach Case," December 9, 2015, https://www.bankinfosecurity.com/wyndham-agrees-to-settle-ftc-breach-case-a-8737.
19. T. Cornell, "Wyndham – A Case Study in Cybersecurity: How the Cost of a Relatively Small Breach Can Rival That of a Major Hack Attack," *Corporate Counsel Business Journal*, March 19, 2015, http://ccbjournal.com/articles/31991/wyndham-%E2%80%93-case-study-cybersecurity-how-cost-relatively-small-breach-can-rival-major-h.
20. "Timeline: The Growing Number of Hotel Data Breaches," *Hotel News Now*, November 30, 2018, http://www.hotelnewsnow.com/Articles/50937/Timeline-The-growing-number-of-hotel-data-breaches.
21. *FTC v. Wyndham Worldwide Corp.*, 799 F. 3d 236 (Court of Appeals, 3rd Circuit 2015).
22. U.S. House of Representatives Committee on Oversight and Government Reform Majority Staff Report, "The Equifax Data Breach," December 2018. The 96-page report gives an excellent summary of the report. Much was also written in the general press (e.g., *New York Times)* and computer press (e.g., *Ars Technica*).

23. Our discussion with references to the literature is in Robert H. Sloan and Richard Warner, *Unauthorized Access: The Crisis in Online Privacy and Information Security* (Boca Raton, FL: Chapman & Hall/CRC Press, 2013).

24. D. Goodin, "Critical Vulnerability under 'Massive' Attack Imperils High-Impact Sites [Updated]," *Ars Technica*, March 9, 2017, https://arstechnica.com/information-technology/2017/03/critical-vulnerability-under-massive-attack-imperils-high-impact-sites/.

25. "Equifax's CEO Who Oversaw Its Huge Data Breach Is Retiring with a $90 Million Pay Day," *Fortune*, accessed December 27, 2018, http://fortune.com/2017/09/26/equifax-ceo-richard-smith-net-worth/.

26. L. Dignan, "Equifax Has Spent $242.7 Million on Its Data Breach So Far," ZDNet, accessed December 27, 2018, https://www.zdnet.com/article/equifax-has-spent-242-7-million-on-its-data-breach-so-far/.

27. D. E. Sanger et al., "Marriott Data Breach Is Traced to Chinese Hackers as U.S. Readies Crackdown on Beijing," *New York Times*, December 12, 2018, https://www.nytimes.com/2018/12/11/us/politics/trump-china-trade.html.

28. Sanger et al.

29. Sanger et al.

30. Reuters, "North Korean Defectors' Personal Data Was Stolen by Hackers, South Says," *New York Times*, December 29, 2018, https://www.nytimes.com/2018/12/28/world/asia/north-korea-defectors-hack.html.

31. K. Zetter, *Countdown to Zero Day: Stuxnet and the Launch of the World's First Digital Weapon* (New York: Crown, 2014).

32. D. E. Sanger and N. Perlroth, "Cyberattack Disrupts Printing of Major Newspapers," *New York Times*, December 31, 2018, https://www.nytimes.com/2018/12/30/business/media/los-angeles-times-cyberattack.html.

33. L. Whitney, "Anthem's Stolen Customer Data Not Encrypted," CNET, February 6, 2015, https://www.cnet.com/news/anthems-hacked-customer-data-was-not-encrypted/.

34. Sanger et al., "Marriott Data Breach Is Traced to Chinese Hackers as U.S. Readies Crackdown on Beijing."

35. "32 Cybersecurity Experts Predict Threats and Trends for 2018," *PhoenixNAP* (blog), accessed January 17, 2019, https://phoenixnap.com/blog/?p=66234.

36. B. Dean et al., "Sorry Consumers, Companies Have Little Incentive to Invest in Better Cybersecurity Quartz," http://qz.com/356274/cybersecurity-breaches-hurt-consumers-companies-not-so-much/ (last visited June 26, 2016).

37. "Underinvesting in Cybersecurity: How Do You Know How Much Security Is Enough?" 2014, http://www.symantec.com/connect/ blogs/underinvesting-cybersecurity-how-do-you-know-how-much-security-enough; Accenture 2013 Global Risk Management Study, Accenture 2013, https://www.accenture.com/us-en/~/ media/Accenture/Conversion-Assets/DotCom/Documents/ Global/PDF/Industries_6/Accenture-Global-Risk-Management-Study-2013.pdf.

38. World Economic Forum, Partnering for Cyber Resilience Towards the Quantification of Cyber Threats World Economic Forum 9 2016, http://www3.weforum.org/docs/WEFUSA_ QuantificationofCyberThreats_Report2015.pdf. A recent Ponemon report reaches similar conclusions. "Measuring & Managing the Cyber Risks to Business Operations," Tenable, December 2018, http://static.tenable.com/marketing/research-reports/Research-Report-Ponemon-Institute-Measuring_and_Managing_the_ Cyber_Risks_to_Business_Operations.pdf.

39. World Economic Forum.

40. On objective and subjective assessment generally, see Z. A. Collier et al., "Cybersecurity Standards: Managing Risk and Creating Resilience," *Computer* 47, no. 9, September 2014: 70–6, https://doi. org/10.1109/MC.2013.448.

41. Software is different from other engineered products in that sufficiently complex software inevitably has some programming flaws. As far back as the 1980s, a panel convened to study the issues with software for President Reagan's Strategic Defense Initiative noted, "Simply because of its inevitable large size, the software capable of performing the battle management task for strategic defense will contain errors. *All systems of useful complexity contain software errors.*" Strategic Def. Initiative Org., Dept of Def., 19980819-140. Eastport Study Group: Summer Study 1985. A Report to the Director, Strategic Initiative Organization 14 1985, available at http://dodreports.com/ada351613 (emphasis added). Recently, Capers Jones noted that one goal of software engineering best practices is to increase the percentage of bugs removed prior to delivery from 85 percent to something that "approach[es] 99 percent," (*not* that it approaches 100%). Jones, *supra* note 114, at xxvi. In contrast, design flaws are not inevitable in, for example, refrigerators, batteries, and bridges even when they exhibit considerable complexity. Software alone combines complexity and inevitable flaws. Thus, no matter how much one invests in

development procedures designed to reduce programming flaws, flaws—and perhaps vulnerabilities—will remain.

42. T. J. Smedinghoff, "Defining the Legal Standard for Information Security: What Does 'Reasonable' Security Really Mean?" in *Securing Privacy in the Internet Age*, eds. Chander, G., Gelman, L., and Radin M. J. (Stanford University Press, 2008), 19–40.

CHAPTER 2

Software Vulnerabilities

W E'LL USE THE TERM *vulnerability* in its technical, information security sense: a weakness that could lead to a security breach. *Software* vulnerabilities are weaknesses of the software, in fact *defects*, that hackers can exploit to gain unauthorized access. Software programs currently contain an unacceptable number of vulnerabilities. As we will discuss, it's possible to write software with many fewer, albeit still some, vulnerabilities.

Since today's rate of software vulnerabilities is high, and since there will always be some software vulnerabilities, all organizations, and especially large organizations, ought to manage their software to defend against attacks. All too often, large corporations such as Wyndham Hotels or Equifax fail to take appropriate security measures to defend adequately. For example, they don't have adequate anti-malware software in place or they don't patch software in a timely manner. We will call these *software management* vulnerabilities. We discuss these vulnerabilities in Chapter 3.

Software engineers know how to minimize (though, alas, not how to totally eliminate) software defects, also known as bugs. The most common and familiar kind of bugs are errors in programming leading to software crashing or giving the wrong result for some expected use from authorized users. The defects we are most concerned about here are (*security*) *vulnerabilities* (also called *security bugs*), by which we mean a defect in software, which can be exploited to gain unauthorized access or privileges.

Software engineering basics, including both how to write individual small computer programs well, and how to combine them into large software systems, is a fairly well-developed subject. The basics of high-quality code construction and software engineering generally form a significant fraction of the required portion of the model computer science bachelor's degree curriculum jointly published by the two main professional societies for computer science both in 2013[1] and in earlier versions.[2] Avoiding security vulnerabilities in particular started getting significant space in the model curriculum in the 2008 version and is prominently featured in the 2013 version.

Years of studies dating back to the 1980s, confirm the common wisdom among experts in software development that proper attention to software development leads to lower defect rates.[3] So, why do software developers not do what they know how to do? Why is software so full of bugs, including vulnerabilities?

DISTRIBUTION OF VULNERABILITIES OVER TYPES OF SOFTWARE

Before answering, we should clarify the question. What we really want to know is: Why is there a relatively small group of very widely installed and commonly used programs that have lots of security vulnerabilities? The security vulnerabilities database CVE Details lists thousands of products that have had at least one reported security vulnerability sometime in the past 20 years. However, a fairly small group of programs is responsible for a wildly disproportionate share of the reported vulnerabilities over the years. These include:[4]

- *Consumer and end-user facing operating systems*: Windows and Mac OS X and Android and iOS (iPhone/iPad operating system); in the 2018 list, Android (both in the Android operating system itself and in underlying Qualcomm firmware) and Microsoft Windows are especially prominent

- *Adobe PDF readers and writers*: In 2018, Adobe DC and Adobe Reader DC, as well as various versions in earlier years

- *Web browsers*: Chrome, Firefox, Internet Explorer, and Safari

- Operating systems used primarily by software professionals (Linux) and server operating systems that would be used by organizations for purposes such as serving their own web pages (various versions of Windows Server and Enterprise Linux server)

- Microsoft Office

- Adobe Flash

A simple count of vulnerabilities only provides an extremely crude idea of which ones will be exploited.[5] Nevertheless, we can see that there are some extremely widely deployed pieces of end-user facing software that have large numbers of vulnerabilities. Indeed, a different methodology found that vulnerabilities exploited in practice are even more concentrated. In both 2015 and 2016, all the top 10 vulnerabilities *used by criminal exploit kits* were found in Adobe and Microsoft products.[6]

SOURCES OF SOFTWARE DEFECTS

The sources of vulnerabilities are generally the same as the sources of defects. Vulnerabilities, after all, are a particular type of software defect, one a hacker can exploit to gain unauthorized access. As the software experts Capers Jones and Oliver Bonsignour note, "Software bugs or defects stem from many sources and have many causes."[7] Our concerns, however, are more limited. We are especially interested in why there are so many defects and what can be done about them. First, though, we want to discuss the reasons for the *inevitability* of defects, and for that purpose, it is sufficient to focus on four sources of defects.

Complexity

Defects are inevitable in sufficiently complex software. As far back as the 1980s, a panel convened to study the issues with software for President Reagan's Strategic Defense Initiative noted, "Simply because of its inevitable large size, the software capable of performing the battle management task for strategic defense will contain errors. *All systems of useful complexity contain software errors* [emphasis added]."[8] As Capers Jones notes, one goal of software engineering best practices is to increase the percentage of bugs removed prior to delivery from 85% to something that "approach[es] 99%," *not* 100%.[9] In contrast, design flaws are *not* inevitable in, for example, refrigerators, batteries, and bridges even when they exhibit considerable complexity. Software alone combines complexity and inevitable flaws. Thus, no matter how much one invests in development procedures designed to reduce programming flaws, flaws—likely including vulnerabilities—will remain.

Computing Progress Adds to Today's Complexity

Consumers demand a variety of different types of software, and within those types, they demand software that performs an increasingly rich and varied number of tasks. Your word processor alone will create a variety of different file formats, proofread what you produce, autocorrect typos, allow you to insert graphics, let you select from a variety of fonts, and so on. Laptops costing only several hundred dollars can run games of remarkable complexity with excellent graphics that can be displayed on large screens. None of this was possible 20 years ago.

One source of the complexity of software is that your computer is a general-purpose machine. It can in theory run whatever can be programmed, which is why back in the 1980s it could already be accurately said that, *"All systems of useful complexity contain software errors."*

However, the rapid increase in computing power over the last 30-plus years ensures that computers can run ever more complex software. To handle the variety of complex programs, a contemporary computer is a very powerful, *very* complex general-purpose machine. A high-end CPU may have billions of transistors. Today's software, ranging from specific applications, through all the infrastructure software on every computer (e.g., the operating system) to all the infrastructure software behind the web, is all vastly more complex than ever before.

Incidentally, there are also vastly more de facto computers running complex software than ever before, and their number is growing at an astonishing rate. This is IoT, which we will discuss in Chapter 6.

Discrete Mathematics: The Difficulty of Over-Engineering for Safety

Software is different from other engineered products in that sufficiently complex software inevitably has programming flaws. Flaws are not inevitable in, for example, the design and manufacture of refrigerators, batteries, or bridges even when they exhibit considerable complexity. Software alone combines complexity and inevitable flaws.

One reason is that most engineering is governed by *continuous* mathematics, whereas software is governed by *discrete* mathematics. Continuous mathematics includes the mathematics of the real numbers, which describes the physics of motion and electricity. Discrete mathematics includes the mathematics of the integers and of strings of letters. For our purposes, the heart of continuous mathematics is the notion of a continuous function. The definition of a continuous function is typically given in calculus classes using Greek lambdas and epsilons, but what a continuous function means to an engineer is that if, in a continuous system, you make a very small error in one of your inputs, the error in the behavior of your system must also be small. The discrete mathematics that governs software offers no such guarantees. An error in a single line of a million-line program can cause arbitrarily large errors.

One consequence is that there is no way to "over-engineer" for safety in designing software, as one can in designing many physical systems. For example, to design a building to withstand 140 mph winds, the calculations about the necessary material strength, thickness, and so on, to withstand 150 mph winds need to be done, and then it should be built according to those calculations, thus creating an extra margin for safety. There are analogous things to do in many engineering situations but not in the construction of software.

The Consumer Demand for Insecure Software

Complexity and discrete mathematics account for some software defects. However, even within those limits, software engineers could create far more secure software than they typically do today. Why don't they?

The fundamental reason is that reducing defects, including vulnerabilities, generally requires a longer and more costly development process. Consumers have been unwilling to pay for the added value of security through slightly higher retail prices, and companies dependent on consumer sales don't offer what consumers don't want. "Businesses are profit-making ventures, so they make decisions based on both short- and long-term profitability,"[10] and the "market often rewards first-to-sell and lowest cost rather than extra time and cost in development."[11] The typical profit-maximizing strategy is to keep costs down and be the first to offer a particular type of software, even if it is imperfect in a variety of ways, including having vulnerabilities.[12]

This is the profit-maximizing strategy because the damage caused by software vulnerabilities is a negative externality for software manufacturers. As we discussed in Chapter 1, negative externalities warp market incentives. Since they do not bear the loss, profit-driven businesses do not invest time, effort, and money in eliminating negative externalities such as vulnerabilities. Such investment would just reduce profits.

Society as a whole would clearly be better off if software developers did make some investment in reducing vulnerabilities. Developing software with fewer vulnerabilities would consume less time, effort, and money than the billions we lose from unauthorized access. In short, society as a whole would make more efficient use of our economic resources if there were no negative externality.

We can end the externality in two ways: use legal regulation or wait for buyers to change their attitudes and demand secure software. However, buyers might not be able to demand secure software since they might be unable to tell if software is secure. We discuss this issue later in this chapter in the section on lemons markets. Legal regulation can end the externality by requiring software developers to compensate buyers for losses caused by vulnerabilities. The legal requirement of compensation is a way to make buyers' losses impose corresponding losses on developers. When legal enforcement is sufficiently widespread and certain, profit-driven developers have an incentive to invest in reducing vulnerabilities.

THE "MAKE THEM LIABLE" REMEDY FOR SOFTWARE VULNERABILITIES AND ITS LIMITS

Many endorse the following remedy to software vulnerabilities: make software manufacturers liable for the damage caused by hackers when they exploit software vulnerabilities to gain unauthorized access to computers and networks.[13] The two core ideas are straightforward: (1) It is unreasonable for manufacturers to produce vulnerability-ridden software when they know how to reduce vulnerabilities, and (2) give them an incentive to behave more reasonably by making them liable for producing vulnerability-ridden software. We consider three legal options for implementing this idea: strict liability, negligence liability, and liability for defective product design.

Strict Liability

Strict liability makes you responsible for losses you cause, even if the loss was not your fault. Strict liability would impose the entire cost of software vulnerabilities on software developers. The difficulty is that software vulnerabilities differ fundamentally from the type of case in which the law typically imposes strict liability.

Classic examples of strict liability are inherently dangerous activities. Keeping wild animals is an example. Keep wild animals and you are strictly liable for the harm they cause. To compare software, first note that when you keep wild animals, you can take precautions to prevent the harm, *and the more precautions you take, the more the risk of harm decreases.* Although you cannot completely eliminate the risk, you can make it as small as you like. You could keep your tigers in a cage within a cage, with top-of-the-line locks, 24-hour electronic monitoring, and as many round-the-clock human guards as you chose. You will eventually decide, at some point, that the time, effort, and money required for increased precautions are not worth the degree of risk reduction they offer, but the point is you have the choice.

Software developers don't have that choice. They cannot drive risks arbitrarily close to zero by spending larger and larger sums. There will always be some security vulnerabilities in any system. No matter what they do, in sufficiently complex programs enough vulnerabilities will remain to create a significant risk of loss. Compare this to keeping wild animals. Suppose that the animals would escape once a month—no matter how careful you were. How many people would keep animals if they faced once-a-month liability for the harm they would cause? Zoos might, but visiting them would be very costly since their fees would have to generate enough money to cover the amounts they would constantly pay out in compensation (or in insurance premiums). Strict liability could create this situation for software vulnerabilities. It would significantly discourage the sale of existing software and the development of new programs. Only where developers could charge enough to cover their inevitable liability would they offer software for sale. This is a highly undesirable outcome in a world now highly dependent on digital technology and on its continued development and refinement.

We can avoid the problems that confront strict liability by making software developers liable for only the losses caused by *some* vulnerabilities, not all of them. This is what negligence liability and liability for defective design do.

Negligence Liability

To avoid negligence liability, you must act reasonably. If you fail to do so, you are liable for the losses caused by the foreseeable harms of your actions. Thus, a software developer would be liable in negligence for losses resulting from a vulnerability only if the vulnerability was a foreseeable result of the developer's failure to act as a reasonable developer would. Our main objection to negligence liability is that it only sufficiently reduces software vulnerabilities if it is combined with a solution to the lack of information problem we discussed in the previous chapter. We argue for this point in the next section.

Another difficulty with negligence liability is that determining what is reasonable behavior for creating low-defect software behavior can be tricky because of the inevitability of some software defects. That difficulty, though real, is almost certainly overstated by major software producers.

Liability for Defective Product Design

You are liable for defective product design when the use of the product involves a foreseeable and unreasonable risk of harm. Holding software developers liable for defective design would create an incentive for developers to adopt vulnerability-reducing development techniques and procedures, as long as courts hold that not adopting them creates a foreseeable and unreasonable risk of harm. Given the references to foreseeability and unreasonableness, you may well wonder how liability for defective design differs from negligence liability. The answer lies in the application and interpretation of foreseeability and unreasonableness in the specific context of product design. For our purposes, we need not pursue that issue. Our objection to defective design liability is the same as our objection to negligence liability. It will only sufficiently reduce software vulnerabilities if it is combined with a solution to the lack of information problem.

LACK OF INFORMATION ABOUT COSTS AND PROBABILITIES

To see the problem, consider that the law cannot simply tell software developers to "invest more." That would be like telling students they must write a paper of a certain number of pages to get a passing grade but not telling them how many pages. Some would write too little; some, too much. The same would happen with software. Some developers would invest too much; some, too little. Ideally, we want developers to offer buyers software options that, when embedded in the overall system, yield a combination of defensive measures that best minimizes the sum of the cost of the defensive measures and all the expected losses with those defensive measures. The problem is the lack of information needed to estimate the expected loss avoided for a given company from adopting a type of defense against a type of data breach. When courts cannot give businesses a sufficiently clear indication of what they should do instead of following prevailing industry practices, it is quite difficult to convince a court that a business that followed those practices acted unreasonably.[14] Standard negligence liability will not create a sufficient incentive to adopt vulnerability-reducing development practices.

Essentially, the same arguments lead to the same conclusion for product liability for defective design. A product is defective in design when its use involves a foreseeable and unreasonable risk of harm. Holding software developers liable for defective design would create an incentive for developers to adopt vulnerability-reducing development techniques and procedures, as long as the courts held that not adopting them would create an foreseeable and unreasonable risk of harm. However, holding developers to this standard would not provide an adequate incentive to reduce vulnerabilities. The reason is the same as in the negligence case: following existing custom and practice is evidence of reasonableness, and, as a practical matter, it is difficult to overcome a business's claim that followed the prevailing industry practices and hence acted reasonably.[15] Extreme cases aside, it is unlikely that courts will hold that not adopting vulnerability-reducing development techniques and procedures creates an unreasonable risk of harm.

Our critique of negligence and products liability applies to any standard that incorporates a reasonableness requirement for software development where the courts will rely primarily on custom and prevailing industry practice to define what counts as "reasonable." Relying on reasonableness requirements is nonetheless quite common. As information security law expert Tom Smedinghoff notes, "Laws and regulations rarely specify the security measures a business should implement to satisfy its legal obligations. Most simply obligate companies to establish and maintain 'reasonable' or 'appropriate' security measures, controls, safeguards, or procedures, but give no further direction or guidance."[16]

To avoid misunderstanding, we should emphasize that we are by no means rejecting relying on legal regulation that imposes reasonableness requirements. Quite the contrary, we will propose such regulation in the chapters that follow. We address the lack of information problem in the next chapter. In the case of software vulnerabilities, however, there is an attractive alternative. Legal liability focuses on changing the behavior of businesses. There is another option: change the behavior of consumers.

CHANGING CONSUMER DEMAND

If enough consumers demanded more secure, less vulnerability-ridden software, profit-driven businesses would provide it. But how does one change what consumers currently demand? Our answer, which we have worked out elsewhere, argues for the creation of a market norm under which software developers offer adequately secure software. We show how a combination of legal regulation and education can make it the norm for consumers to demand sufficiently secure software.[17] But, one might well ask, what about the lack of information problem?

After all, sufficiently secure software is software that adequately promotes the business and consumer risk management goals. We've argued that meeting those risk management goals *requires* information about costs and probabilities. So how could a process of legal regulation and education to change norms generate the necessary information? It can't. We explain how to generate the necessary information in Chapter 4. We conclude this chapter by considering another problem that appears to confront our "consumer demand" proposal.

A LEMONS MARKET FOR SOFTWARE?

Our proposal that we should rely on the norm that consumers demand sufficiently secure software requires that consumers be able to tell secure from insecure software. Can they? The stakes are high. If they cannot, the result is a "lemons market" in which only insecure software is available. We explain a lemons market, then consider whether consumers can tell secure from insecure software.

We explain a lemons market using a version of the "used car" example first employed by the economist George Akerlof in his seminal article, "The Market for Lemons."[18] Suppose a town has 300 used cars for sale: 100 good ones worth $6,000, 100 so-so ones worth $4,000, and 100 lemons worth $2,000. Buyers cannot tell the difference between a good and bad car; thus, buying a used car means entering a lottery in which the buyer has a 1/3 chance of getting a good car, a 1/3 chance of getting a so-so car, and a 1/3 chance of getting a lemon. The expected value of that purchase is $4,000, so rational buyers will be willing to pay at most $4,000. Sellers who value their good cars at over $4,000 will not offer those good cars for sale, so the market will contain only lemons worth $2,000 and not-so-good cars worth $4,000. As a result, the expected value of a used car drops to $3,000, so rational buyers will not pay more than $3,000 for a car, and now sellers who value their cars above $3,000 do not offer them for sale, and thus only the lemons are left on the market. In general, a lemons market exists when four conditions are fulfilled: (1) the products on the market vary significantly in quality, that is, the extent to which they have certain properties that buyers are willing to pay more for; (2) buyers cannot discriminate among products with different degrees of quality, but sellers can at least partially distinguish them; (3) there is no reliable signal of quality (i.e., sellers with an excellent car have no way to reliably disclose this fact to buyers); and (4) buyers know there is a mix of products on the market.

Are these four conditions fulfilled for software vulnerabilities?

In answering this question, it is important to distinguish between two markets: the market for *security software and systems* (such as firewalls, antivirus software, or secure USB memory sticks), and the market for other sorts of mass-consumer software. Bruce Schneier has argued convincingly that the former market is a lemons market.[19] Others have picked up on his claim and argued that it may also apply to *software that is (relatively) secure*—that is, software which is relatively free of vulnerabilities.[20] We are not so sure. While there are strong arguments that *security software* is a lemons market, it is unclear whether *secure* software is a lemons market. Conditions (2) and (4) are arguably fulfilled, but (1) and (3) are problematic. We first briefly review the arguments in favor of regarding conditions (2) and (4) as being fulfilled. Condition (2): Typical consumers do not have the expertise to distinguish by inspecting the software between secure and insecure software,[21] while the developers do know something about what production practices they are using. Condition (4): Buyers—or at least a significant portion of buyers—do know that the market contains both vulnerability-ridden and not so vulnerability-ridden software.[22]

Condition (1) requires (in part) that buyers be willing to pay more for software with few vulnerabilities than for similar vulnerability-ridden software. At the moment, this is not true. Buyers are, on the whole, *not* willing to pay more for more secure software.

Condition (3) requires that there do not exist any reliable signals that differentiate vulnerability-ridden from similar software with significantly fewer vulnerabilities. Typical consumers do not have the expertise to distinguish *by inspecting the software* between vulnerability-ridden software and software with significantly fewer vulnerabilities. Inspection is not, however, the only way to determine the extent to which software suffers from vulnerabilities. The general quality of the software is a moderately reliable signal of the extent to which it contains vulnerabilities. Vulnerabilities are a kind of flaw, or defect, in the software, and it is reasonable to assume that their occurrence correlates with the occurrence of other flaws, such as a tendency to crash or give wrong answers. Indeed, it is routine not to distinguish sharply between defects and vulnerabilities. As security experts observed back in 2004, "Software *defects* are the single most critical weakness in computer systems …. [S]oftware defects lead directly to software exploit[ation]."[23] The correlation between vulnerabilities and defects is sufficiently strong that at least some buyers will infer that improperly functioning software is likely to contain significant vulnerabilities. This signaling mechanism is far from perfect, but sufficient detection does not require that all or most buyers detect vulnerability-ridden software, just that enough do to impose losses on sellers who offer such software. Thus, there is very possibly a signaling mechanism that is strong enough to prevent a lemons market.

If this signaling mechanism is not enough, there are other ways to create the required signal. These include warranties (signaling the manufacturer's confidence that the software is secure), industry standards (compliance signals that the software is secure), consumer protection laws (compliance signals that the software is secure), and product certification (signals the certifier's confidence that the software is secure).

ARTIFICIAL INTELLIGENCE: A FUTURE SOLUTION?

If we could teach a machine learning system what a software defect looks like, the system could run through millions of lines of code looking for the patterns indicative of defects. We do not yet know how to teach a system what a defect looks like, but there is academic work on that topic.[24] If sufficiently cheap and accurate machine learning detection became a standard part of software development, that could greatly reduce the number of software defects (and thus vulnerabilities). Bruce Schneier imagines a future in which we would say, "Remember those years when software vulnerabilities were a thing, before ML [machine learning] vulnerability finders were built into every compiler and fixed them before the software was ever released? Wow, those were crazy years."[25] For now, however, and for the immediate future, significant software defects are the reality.

CONCLUSION

The next chapter turns to security management vulnerabilities. The "change consumer demand" approach we suggest for software vulnerabilities will not work for security management vulnerabilities. We suggest legal liability for mismanagement instead. The suggestion opens us to our own objection that we lack the information about costs and probabilities necessary for fully effective legal regulation. We address this problem in Chapter 4.

ENDNOTES

1. The Joint Task Force on Computing Curricula, Association for Computing Machinery (ACM), IEEE Computer Society, "Computer Science Curricula 2013: Curriculum Guidelines for

Undergraduate Degree Programs in Computer Science," December 20, 2013, https://dl.acm.org/citation.cfm?id=2534860.

2. See, e.g., E. Roberts et al., *Computing Curricula 2001: Computer Science* (IEEE Computer Society Press, 2001).
3. For example, I. J. Hayes, "Applying Formal Specification to Software Development in Industry," *IEEE Transactions on Software Engineering* SE-11, no. 2, 1985: 169–78; A. MacCormack et al., "Trade-Offs between Productivity and Quality in Selecting Software Development Practices," *IEEE Software* 20, no. 5, 2003: 78–85.
4. "Top 50 Products Having Highest Number of CVE Security Vulnerabilities," accessed December 30, 2018, https://www.cvedetails.com/top-50-products.php.
5. K. Nayak et al., "Some Vulnerabilities Are Different Than Others," in *International Workshop on Recent Advances in Intrusion Detection* (Springer, 2014), 426–446.
6. "New Kit, Same Player: Top 10 Vulnerabilities Used by Exploit Kits in 2016," accessed January 3, 2019, https://www.recordedfuture.com/top-vulnerabilities-2016/.
7. C. Jones and O. Bonsignour, *The Economics of Software Quality* (Upper Saddle River, NJ: Addison-Wesley Professional, 2011).
8. Strategic Def. Initiative Org., Dept of Def., 19980819-140. Eastport Study Group: Summer Study 1985. A Report to the Director, Strategic Initiative Organization 14, 1985, available at http://www.dtic.mil/dtic/tr/fulltext/u2/a169210.pdf.
9. C. Jones, *Software Engineering Best Practices: Lessons from Successful Projects in the Top Companies* (New York: McGraw-Hill, 2010), xxvi.
10. B. Schneier, "Information Security and Externalities," *Schneier on Security* (blog), January 2007, https://www.schneier.com/essays/archives/2007/01/information_security_1.html.
11. E. H. Spafford, *Remembrances of Things Pest*, 53 Comm. ACM 35, no. 36, 2010.
12. See generally, C. Shapiro and H. R. Varian, "Information Rules: A Strategic Guide to the Network Economy," 50–51, 1999. The economics and information security community has developed Shapiro and Varian's initial insights. Much of this work has been reported in the annual Workshop on the Economics of Information Security since 2002, https://econinfosec.org/. For a good early survey, see R. Anderson and T. Moore, "Information Security: Where Computer Science, Economics and Psychology Meet," *367 Phil. Transactions Royal Soc'y A* 2717, 2009: 2721–22.

13. Bruce Schneier has been a prominent advocate of this view. *See* B. Schneier, "Liability Changes Everything," *Schneier on Security* (blog), November 2003, http://www.schneier.com/essay-025. html, and B. Schneier, *Click Here to Kill Everybody: Security and Survival in a Hyper-Connected World* (New York: W. W. Norton & Company, 2018).

14. Egregiously bad programming practices are sometimes an exception.

15. Evidence of industry practices is relevant under both of the main tests used to determine defectiveness—the "risk/utility test" (a product is defective when its risk of harm exceeds its benefits), and the "consumer expectations" test (a product is defective when it fails to meet the reasonable expectations of consumers).

16. T. J. Smedinghoff, "Defining the Legal Standard for Information Security: What Does 'Reasonable' Security Really Mean?" in *Securing Privacy in the Internet Age*, eds. Chander, G., Gelman, L., and Radin M. J. (Stanford University Press, 2008), 19–40.

17. R. H. Sloan and R. Warner, *Unauthorized Access: The Crisis in Online Privacy and Information Security* (Boca Raton, FL: Chapman & Hall/CRC Press, 2013).

18. G. A. Akerlof, "The Market for 'Lemons': Quality Uncertainty and the Market Mechanism," *Quarterly Journal of Economics* 84, no. 3, 1970: 488–500.

19. B. Schneier, "How Security Companies Sucker Us with Lemons," *Wired*, April 19, 2007, http://www.wired.com/politics/security/commentary/securitymatters/2007/04/securitymatters_0419.

20. See D. Barnes, "Deworming the Internet," *Texas Law Review* 83, no. 1, 2004.

21. B. Schneier, "How Security Companies Sucker Us with Lemons," *Wired*, April 19, 2007, https://www.wired.com/2007/04/securitymatters-0419/.

22. R. W. Hahn and Anne Layne-Farrar, "The Law and Economics of Software Security," *Harvard Journal of Law & Public Policy* 30, 2006: 302.

23. G. Hoglund and G. McGraw, *Exploiting Software: How to Break Code* (Addison-Wesley Professional, 2004). These lines come at the end of an introductory section of the book that moves from discussing famous software defects that had nothing to do with security and attackers to discussing defects that constitute security holes. Two examples of non-security defects the authors give are NASA's 1999 Mars lander software failure, where a metric versus

English units error caused the loss of the $165 million system and the Denver International Airport automated baggage handling system fiasco.

24. J. J. Kronjee, "Discovering Vulnerabilities Using Data-Flow Analysis and Machine Learning" (Master's Thesis, Open University, 2018), https://dspace.ou.nl/bitstream/1820/9725/1/Kronjee%20J%20 IM9906%20AF%20scriptie.pdf.

25. B. Schneier, "Machine Learning to Detect Software Vulnerabilities," *Schneier on Security* (blog), January 15, 2019, https://www.schneier. com/blog/archives/2019/01/machine_learnin.html.

CHAPTER 3

(Mis)Management

Failing to Defend against Technical Attacks

I N THE LAST CHAPTER, we discussed security weaknesses that arise from weaknesses in the software that organizations, and, indeed, everyone, obtains from third parties. In this chapter, we move to security weaknesses caused by an organization's having inadequate technical defenses for its own computers and networks.

A good metaphor for computer and network security is securing a sports arena. Suppose you are newly in charge of security at United Center where the Chicago Bulls play basketball and the Chicago Blackhawks play hockey. You would find out where the doors are, lock the ones you don't need, post guards at the rest to check credentials (tickets, press passes, etc.), and put guards inside to monitor behavior. Computer and network security is similar. You shut down access points, post "credential check guards" to verify authorization (passwords, two-factor identification, and so on), and monitor for improper behavior with systems ranging from home computer antivirus programs to multimillion-dollar systems defending corporate networks. One important dissimilarity is that large organizations have much more control over the structure of a network than even the Chicago Bulls' management does over the layout of the United Center. They cannot, practically speaking, wall off the first 10 rows of seats at the United Center even if that would improve security, but organizations can partition a network to isolate particularly sensitive information and applications in ways that minimize the chance of unauthorized access. In general, systems administrators know—or should know—how to reduce vulnerabilities and how to defend against attacks on vulnerabilities that are present. However, we often see something very different in practice.

In this chapter, we will discuss the inadequate defenses seen in practice against technical attacks on software vulnerabilities and on networks, leaving the discussion of attacks on human vulnerabilities, such as phishing, for Chapter 7. The focus of this chapter also differs from that of the previous chapter. Our concern in Chapter 2 was with developing commercial (and open-source) software with dramatically fewer defects. We are concerned with software in this chapter too, but only to the extent that it is embedded in a business's network. Our focus is on defending the vulnerabilities that are there, and the certainty that some of them *will* be attacked.

To organize our discussion, we break weaknesses into categories, but be aware that the categories overlap at the edges. As one example, it is bad practice for a medium or large organization not to have any firewalls. One might classify that bad practice either as introducing the vulnerability of not having a firewall, or as failing to respond to the unavoidable vulnerability of making some of the organization's computers, such as its web servers, partly accessible to outsiders. As a second example, consider the term "network security" itself. Some IT professionals use that term to mean preventing and monitoring unauthorized access to an organization's network. Others extend that definition to unauthorized access to a network or network-accessible resources.

In other words, to more or less all of the security issues we are concerned with here.

How we organize our exact categories of vulnerabilities and defenses, large organizations should surely be on notice that there are criminals looking to steal data for profit, as well as occasional cases of nation-state espionage. Fifteen or 20 years ago, hacking may have been primarily a matter of vandalism, but those days are long past. At least since the massive breach of TJX (the retailer that operates TJ Maxx and Marshalls, among others) in late 2006, big data breaches have been in the news. So, given that software contains vulnerabilities, large organizations should be employing some level of defenses against breaches. However, in most breaches where the details of how the breach occurred become public, we see that seriously inadequate defense was a contributing factor and sometimes the main factor.

Although the security landscape is ever changing, the basics of defense have been known for years.[1] There are several sets of guidelines on how to defend for organizations. We'll consider two particularly well-respected ones: The Center for Internet Security's (CIS) CIS Controls V7[2] and the Australian government's Australian Cyber Security Centre's (ACSC) Essential Eight strategies to mitigate cybersecurity incidents.[3] We'll discuss the current version of these guidelines, but neither is brand new. Versions of the CIS Critical Security Controls (earlier called "SANS" rather than "CIS") have been around since 2009.[4]

(MIS)MANAGING SOFTWARE VULNERABILITIES

As we have discussed, the current rate of software defects is quite high, and some nonzero rate of defects is inevitable. Furthermore, we might expect the rate of software vulnerabilities to be higher than the rate of other defects, such as a bug that makes a program crash on certain inputs. To minimize the occurrence of this type of non-security defect, software engineers must ensure that systems can withstand mistaken inputs from careless or confused users. To minimize software *security vulnerabilities*, however, software engineers must ensure that systems can withstand deliberately chosen malicious inputs designed by intelligent adversaries.

We will now discuss three broad categories of defending against software vulnerabilities: patching software promptly, whitelisting software on critical computers, and running appropriate antivirus software. A recurring theme as we discuss both these defenses and others later is that each form of defense helps tremendously in some situations, but not in others. The information security principle that a big organization should be using several different forms of defense is referred to as *defense in depth*.

KEEPING SOFTWARE UPDATED AND ACCOUNTED FOR: PATCHING AND INVENTORYING

Maintaining an accurate and complete inventory of deployed software and updating that software promptly figures prominently in both the CIS Controls and the ACSC Essential Eight. In professional IT management circles, any update to software to fix defects in the software is called a *patch*, and installing those updates is called *patching*. For example, Microsoft issues patches for both Windows and Office almost every month, and usually many of the defects those patches fix are security vulnerabilities.

Two of the Essential Eight strategies are promptly installing patches for applications and promptly installing patches for operating systems. Those two strategies were two of *four* in an earlier 2013 version that called for only four vulnerability mitigation strategies. The Essential Eight calls for patching within 48 hours for the case of "extreme risk" vulnerabilities. The CIS Top 20 Critical Security Controls (CSC) break out 6 of the 20 as fundamental controls, that is, the ones organizations should implement first. One of those fundamental controls is to inventory software in use, and another is "continuous vulnerability management," which includes patching as an important component.

Failure to Patch

Of the three famous breaches that we examined in depth (excluding the Marriott breach, because little is known about its causes at the time of this writing), failure to patch was the main cause of one, and may have been a factor in all three. Failure to patch almost certainly played a role in the Wyndham breaches, as Wyndham simply didn't patch software on a regular basis.

Failure to patch may also have played a role in the Target breach. We know that the hackers stole a username and password from Fazio Mechanical Services and used those credentials to log in to Target's vendor portal. We also know that somehow the attackers were able to move from that vendor portal into the heart of Target's system. We can speculate that there were known unpatched vulnerabilities in Target's system. We also know that malware was eventually installed on Target's POS (point of sale) systems, so the same argument about possible failure to patch applies there.

Finally, failure to patch for months—after multiple notifications—was the main cause of the Equifax breach. As we discussed in the first chapter, Equifax was notified of a critical vulnerability in Apache Struts software and of a patch for it by the Apache Software Foundation on March 7, 2017, and by Department of Homeland Security's (DHS) United States Computer Emergency Readiness Team (US-CERT) on March 8. Equifax didn't patch until the end of July. Equifax *did* do a system scan for the presence of the affected software on March 15, but that scan didn't find the Apache Struts software that was in fact deployed on a publicly facing Equifax system, apparently because they scanned the wrong directory.[5] Equifax clearly lacked both an inventory of its deployed software and an adequate mechanism for applying even highly critical patches. Recall from Chapter 1, that failure to patch this one very serious defect was the direct cause of a breach of over half the U.S. adult population's data, including names, dates of birth, *and* Social Security numbers.

Application Whitelisting

We began with patching for two reasons. First, patching failures have contributed to many breaches. Second, we expect the idea of updating software in response to updates released by Apple, Microsoft, Adobe, and so on, to be familiar to almost all readers from their own experience with their laptops. Application whitelisting may not be as familiar, because it would be unusual for a laptop for personal use. Application whitelisting means having a list of all the approved, trusted programs that may be run on a particular machine, and preventing all other software from running. Application whitelisting is the *first* of the ACSC's Essential Eight and one of CIS's six fundamental controls.

Application whitelisting prevents *any* non-approved software from executing, and could potentially stop the vast majority of data breaches. Whitelisting might sometimes be a minor nuisance or worse if it were used on, say, the work computer of a researcher or analyst, but it is especially appropriate for a POS system, such as Target's. One *really* doesn't want arbitrary software running on one's cash registers in a store! Application whitelisting for Target's POS systems would have stopped the hacker's software from running and prevented the breach.

Malware Defenses

Next, we come to the category that includes the traditional antivirus software that most computer users have been aware of for years. Antivirus software stops malware from running. More precisely, it stops whatever malware is in the defense software's current catalog of currently *known* malware from running. We'll generally use the somewhat more common term "antivirus" rather than "anti-malware" for this software, even though it protects against some types of malware that most security experts would not include in their definition of virus (e.g., worms and Trojans). Malware defense is CIS's Critical Security Control #8.

Antivirus software may or may not have helped Wyndham to prevent the first of the three breaches. The malware installed to scrape and remove data in the first breach may have been new. However, the *same malware* was used in the second attack, so adequate malware defense should certainly have identified and stopped it.

In the case of the Target breach, we discussed that the vendor Fazio Mechanical Services was not running professional caliber anti-malware software that constantly updates its catalog of known malware. Fazio's computer was compromised by known malware that wasn't stopped by the free consumer-grade virus scanning software Fazio was using but would have been stopped by normal quality commercial software. Fazio, as a small business, should have been running commercial antivirus software. But Target also bears some responsibility. As a Fortune 100 company, Target could have required its vendors to use commercial virus-checking software on any systems they used to interact with Target.

Antivirus software is limited, because it only helps with already cataloged malware. It would *not* have helped Target avoid the breach to have antivirus software running on its POS systems, because the malware installed there to scrape and exfiltrate the credit card numbers was a brand new variant of previously seen malware to extract data from POS systems, and no commercial antivirus system recognized the new variant at the time of the Target breach.[6]

DATA DEFENSE: ENCRYPTION

It's been clear for years now that hackers will sometimes successfully break into systems, whether because of weaknesses in software, networks, people, or a combination of all three. *Encrypting sensitive information at rest,* that is, on a computer (as opposed to in transit over the Internet) means that stolen data is valueless to the thieves. Stealing "Robert H. Smith, SSN: 123-45-6789" is valuable; stealing "f1*e;j289sR7!2, SSN: 2@# 29%TGN" is worthless (as long as you don't have the decryption key). CIS Critical Security Control #14, "Controlled Access Based on Need to Know," includes encrypting sensitive data at rest.

Many breaches involve a failure to encrypt personal information at rest. Names, dates of birth, credit card numbers, Social Security numbers, and other personally identifiable information (PII) are stored without encrypting them. None of the Equifax PII that was stolen was encrypted.[7] At the time of this writing, it has just been reported that Marriott did not encrypt its guests' passport numbers.[8] Given the data that Wyndham's hackers obtained, Wyndham surely didn't encrypt its guests' PII.

There are limits to the power of encryption. Encryption works only so long as the hacker who steals the encrypted data doesn't also steal the key. Highly personal information was stolen from the U.S. Office of Personnel Management (OPM) in a 2014 breach: completed answers to the very detailed questionnaires that people fill in to obtain a U.S. security clearance. OPM stored those filled-in forms *unencrypted*. OPM was criticized by security experts for not encrypting this data, but OPM argued that hackers had likely stolen user credentials that would have allowed hackers access to decryption keys had the data been encrypted.[9]

Encryption at rest can be difficult to implement in a meaningful way if a large number of people in the organization need the unencrypted data. We can imagine that in some countries Marriott might need to verify the passport data it has on file at every check-in, meaning very many frontline, non-IT employees around the world would need access to the unencrypted data.

An encryption failure played a significant role in the Target breach, but it wasn't exactly a matter of encrypting data at rest. Target's problem was that they should have encrypted credit card numbers immediately upon cards being swiped at the POS, instead of waiting to encrypt until the information was being transmitted out of the POS for a credit check.

(MIS)MANAGING NETWORK DEFENSES

Now we turn from defenses primarily on individual computers to defenses of networks. In terms of United Center at the beginning of this chapter, we'll now talk about guards at several locations: at the entrance to the United Center itself, and at the entrance point to various critical interior rooms, ranging from the players' changing rooms to the room where ticket sellers store the cash received.

Before we discuss specific defenses, let us return to the issue of complexity that we discussed in terms of software complexity in Chapter 2. Networks suffer from complexity too. In a large organization, both the routers and internal structure of the network can be quite complex, and the more complex the network, the more likely a misjudgment that creates a vulnerability. Complexity is the enemy of security, as many have observed.[10]

We begin with a defense that the general public is aware of today, multifactor authentication, and then move on to other network defenses.

Multifactor Authentication

Multifactor authentication means requiring multiple things from a user wishing to authenticate themselves instead of only a password. The most common form uses two factors, a password plus a code which is texted to the user's phone. Alternatives to the texted code include security tokens and biometrics. As with every defensive measure we discuss, multifactor authentication alone is not a silver bullet. However, stronger user authentication makes it harder for adversaries to use stolen passwords and usernames. Multifactor authentication for both remote access and administrative privileges is one of the ACSC Essential Eight. The CIS Critical Security Controls have multifactor authentication in two places, as part of "Controlled Use of Administrative Privileges" (one of the fundamental six) and as part of "Account Monitoring and Control."

If Target had required multifactor authentication for remote access, including remote access by vendors, the criminals who stole Fazio's login credentials would probably never have gotten into Target's vendor portal. Additionally, we know that at some point the criminals gained access to Target's POS system and almost certainly administrative access. If multifactor authentication was required for administrative access, that too might have stopped the criminals. It is especially important to protect administrative accounts. In computer security, they are the keys to the kingdom.

The Wyndham breaches took place in 2008 and 2009, at a time when multifactor authentication existed, but wasn't nearly as common as it is today. However, this is irrelevant, because Wyndham failed to have even the most basic password security: ensuring that passwords were not common words or really short. One of the ways that Wyndham was breached was by brute-force guessing of simple passwords. Moreover, in some systems, Wyndham left the original default usernames and passwords in place.[11]

Boundary Defenses: Firewalls and Intrusion Detection Systems

The high-level goal is to limit the flow of information at a number of different points: at the machine–network boundary, at the boundary between the organization's networks and the Internet as a whole, and at boundaries between different internal networks with different levels of access and trust. The general public needs to access the organization's website, a much smaller group of people should be able to gain access to websites for vendors, and a *much* smaller group of people should be able to gain access to the organization's internal network for its own employees.

Several CIS Critical Security Controls touch on these, but we'll restrict our attention to the main point, Critical Security Control #11, "Boundary Defense," which calls for inventorying all network boundaries, and using appropriate firewalls and intrusion detection systems at all those boundaries.

Wyndham, remarkably, had no firewalls at all. By 2008, that was egregious misbehavior. Having the *proper* network segregation and firewalls for a large organization is harder. Target, in the aftermath of the breach, repeatedly pointed out that they had spent a lot of money on security and were running firewalls. However, strict firewall rules limiting traffic flows at critical boundaries might have stopped the attack at various points. It might, for example, have disrupted the criminals' command and control communication with their malware. However, the top issue in this area with the Target breach is the ignored alarms from the FireEye systems.

SO HOW HARD IS IT FOR A LARGE ORGANIZATION TO MOUNT A GOOD TECHNICAL DEFENSE?

Wyndham had almost no defenses whatsoever in place. Target and Equifax did take various security measures but not enough, or not well enough, to prevent massive breaches. It's likely that the same is true for Marriott, although it is too soon to say. Diligent attention to either the Essential Eight or to 10 or so of the CIS Critical Security Controls would have prevented these breaches and many more data breaches of other organizations.

This is *not* a matter of simply buying some antivirus software and an entry-level firewall, as a small business might do. Hackers "are well aware of network ... security mechanisms, and are developing increasingly sophisticated and effective methods for subverting them."[12] Both Target and Equifax had firewalls in place, and in both breaches, part of the overall attack involved exploiting vulnerabilities to move data through a firewall.[13]

Implementing all those security controls well requires either having a large enough knowledgeable professional IT staff or outsourcing to a security firm that does as we discuss in Chapter 5; it's not something that is realistic for a small company of a hundred employees, including one or two "IT guys," to do on its own. Indeed, it may not even be reasonable for a 1,500-employee law firm to do on its own.

However, all of Wyndham, Target, Equifax, and Marriott *are Fortune 500 companies*, as are Anthem and Home Depot. The U.S. Office of Personnel Management is a major federal agency with over 5,000 employees. Following 8 or even 20 detailed technical recommendations should be well within the capacity of each of those organizations.

CREATING AN INCENTIVE TO MANAGE BETTER

Current management of defenses fails to adequately approximate both the business and consumer risk management goals. What is the best way to give businesses a stronger incentive to do so? What about the "consumer demand" approach we proposed in Chapter 2 as a way to reduce software vulnerabilities? This approach will not work for mismanagement. There would have to be sufficiently competitive markets in which consumers purchased risk management. Relevant markets typically do not exist. The data aggregator Oracle BlueKai, for example, collects and stores consumer data,[14] but the consumers who are the subjects of that data typically have no market relation with Oracle BlueKai—not unless they are also the data aggregator's customers. One may object that consumers do have market relations in the four examples of data breaches we considered in Chapter 1. Wyndham Hotels, for example, stores information about its hotel customers. However, a relevant market exists only if those customers are sufficiently well informed about hotels' information security practices, and select hotels partly based on their preferences about such practices. The problem, of course, is that consumers are not sufficiently well-informed about the security practices of hotels. Similar remarks hold true for Target, Equifax, and Marriott.

An alternative is to create the needed incentive through legal regulation. This is already happening through the activities of the FTC. "The FTC has brought over fifty security enforcement actions,"[15] including an action against Wyndham Hotels that culminated in the federal court case, *FTC v. Wyndham*, in which the court upheld the FTC's power to enforce security standards under 15 U.S.C. § 45, which prohibits "unfair … practices in or affecting commerce." The FTC was created in 1914 to combat monopolies. In 1938, Congress also gave it a consumer protection role. The idea behind its creation was that the government needs a quick-acting agency with broad investigative powers to reign in big business. The FTC has very broad investigative powers. It can open an investigation against a business whenever it has "reason to believe that any such person, partnership, or corporation has been or is using any unfair method of competition or unfair or deceptive act or practice in or affecting commerce," and "if it shall appear to the Commission that a proceeding by it in respect thereof would be to the interest of the public."[16] If the business and the FTC cannot agree on a resolution of the problems the FTC identifies, the investigation may lead to a federal court case (which is what occurred with Wyndham).

The broad investigative powers of the FTC make it an attractive way to address security mismanagement. Some may object that we should not rely solely on the FTC. FTC investigations are *governmental* actions. Shouldn't *individuals* harmed by security mismanagement also be able to bring legal actions? They can. They can sue under common law negligence theories and under state and federal statutes that require reasonable security. The two regimes work in concert to discipline businesses.

But what about the lack of information problem? The problem is the lack of information needed to estimate the expected loss avoided for a given company from adopting a type of defense against a type of data breach. In Chapter 2, we emphasized the following consequence: When courts cannot give businesses a sufficiently clear indication of what they should do instead of following prevailing industry practices, it is quite difficult to convince a court that a business that followed prevailing practices nonetheless acted unreasonably. The FTC is no different. It will bring actions for inadequate security only in cases of a clear failure to adequately approximate the risk management goals, cases of egregiously bad security like Wyndham. That is indeed just what is seen in the FTC cases.

We need a solution to the lack of information problem. We propose one in the next chapter.

ENDNOTES

1. For example, the first edition of one of the most famous security textbooks came out in 2009: Ross J. Anderson, *Security Engineering: A Guide to Building Dependable Distributed Systems*, 1st ed. (Indianapolis, IN: Wiley, 2001).
2. "CIS Controls V7" (CIS Center for Internet Security, March 19, 2018).
3. Department of Defence, "Strategies to Mitigate Cyber Security Incidents: Australian Signals Directorate (ASD)," accessed December 31, 2018, https://acsc.gov.au/infosec/mitigationstrategies. htm.
4. "SANS Institute—CIS Critical Security Controls: A Brief History," accessed December 31, 2018, https://www.sans.org/ critical-security-controls/history.
5. U.S. House of Representatives Committee on Oversight and Government Reform Majority Staff Report, "The Equifax Data Breach," December 2018.
6. B. Krebbs, "A First Look at the Target Intrusion, Malware," *Krebs on Security* (blog), January 14, 2014, https://krebsonsecurity. com/2014/01/a-first-look-at-the-target-intrusion-malware/.
7. U.S. House of Representatives Committee on Oversight and Government Reform Majority Staff Report, "The Equifax Data Breach."
8. D. E. Sanger, "Marriott Concedes 5 Million Passport Numbers Lost to Hackers Were Not Encrypted," *New York Times*, January 4, 2019, https://www.nytimes.com/2019/01/04/us/politics/marriott-hack-passports.html.
9. A. Boyd, "OPM Breach a Failure on Encryption, Detection," *Federal Times*, August 8, 2017, https://www.federaltimes. com/smr/opm-data-breach/2015/06/19/opm-breach-a-failure-on-encryption-detection/.
10. C.-S. Chan, "Complexity the Worst Enemy of Security," *Computerworld*, December 17, 2012, https://www.computerworld. com/article/2493938/cyberwarfare/complexity-the-worst-enemy-of-security.html.
11. *FTC v. Wyndham Worldwide Corp.*, 799 F. 3d 236 (Court of Appeals, 3rd Circuit 2015).
12. A. Gupta et al., *An Empirical Study of Malware Evolution*, in Communication Systems and Networks Workshops (COMSNETS 2009), 1–10, 1, 2009.

13. Majority Staff Report for Chairman Rockefeller, "A 'Kill Chain' Analysis of the 2013 Target Data Breach" (United States Senate Committee on Commerce, Science, and Transportation, March 6, 2014), 3, https://www.commerce.senate.gov/public/_cache/files/24d3c229-4f2f-405d-b8db-a3a67f183883/23E30AA955B5C00FE57CFD709621592C.2014-0325-target-kill-chain-analysis.pdf; U.S. House of Representatives Committee on Oversight and Government Reform Majority Staff Report, "The Equifax Data Breach," 31.
14. "Oracle Data Cloud: Data Directory," Oracle, n.d., 7.
15. C. J. Hoofnagle, *Federal Trade Commission Privacy Law and Policy* (New York: Cambridge University Press, 2016), 217.
16. 15 U.S.C. §45(b).

CHAPTER 4

A Mandatory Reporting Proposal

S O FAR WE HAVE discussed a lack of adequate information about the likelihood of various sizes of breaches, and problems with inadequate defenses that we have argued are caused by that lack of information. In this chapter, we propose how to obtain the necessary information: by a carefully crafted mandatory reporting requirement.

We begin by returning to the business risk management goal.

THE BUSINESS RISK MANAGEMENT GOAL

Recall from Chapter 1 that the business risk management goal is for a business to employ defensive measures up to the point where the cost of the defensive measures is equal to the expected losses that business avoids by those measures. This is the profit-maximizing strategy, so it would be expected for businesses to strive to meet that goal. However, businesses fail to approximate the risk management goal with regard to business losses for two main reasons: corporate culture and lack of relevant information about breach probabilities and expected losses.

Corporate Culture

Corporate culture has struggled to spend enough on cybersecurity,[1] but this may be changing. According to a recent KMPG study, "Three-quarters [of CEOs] see investment in cybersecurity as an opportunity to find new revenue streams and innovate."[2] However, a 2018 report paints a more negative picture: "Forty-four percent of the 9,500 executives in 122 countries surveyed … say they do not have an overall information security strategy."[3] We assume that corporate culture will eventually embrace the business risk management goal. That will not, however, eliminate the fundamental problem, the lack of information necessary for adequate risk assessment.

Lack of Information

Meeting the business risk management goal requires knowing, or at least estimating, the expected loss avoided by various defensive configurations. The problem is that estimating the expected loss requires reliable information about both the magnitude of the loss and the probability of its occurrence, and sufficient information of that sort is not currently available. Our solution involves mandatory reporting of data breach losses.

MANDATORY REPORTING

We propose closing the information gap by businesses participating in *mandatory* reporting so that the probability of the occurrence of data breaches and their costs to *businesses* can be determined. An *anonymized* summary of the collected information would be shared at least with all mandatory reporters. The anonymized summary of the collected information would provide high-quality information to the business world about the actual prevalence and cost of breaches in practice today.[4] Mandatory sharing has at least two advantages over voluntary sharing. If sharing is voluntary, businesses will weigh the benefits of information sharing with the risks and costs of doing so, and they may decide that the benefits are insufficient. In particular, at the beginning of a voluntary program, an initially small pool of information means limited benefits, and so businesses may be unwilling to participate until enough others do. There may be other ways to overcome these problems, but we will not consider these here. Our concern is to defend mandatory sharing as an acceptable option.

There are at least three existing models that are somewhat similar to what we have in mind. One is the 2015 Cybersecurity Information Sharing Act (CISA),[5] which is voluntary but covers quite similar information. The second is the mandatory reporting of certain electrical outages to the Department of Energy (DOE).[6] Finally, there is the required, completely confidential reporting of network outages to the FCC, under the Network Outage Reporting System (NORS).[7] Each of these three is informative, but none is a perfect match. CISA is voluntary. The DOE reporting covers a much smaller number of incidents than any estimates of the current number of computer security incidents. For example, the public summary of electric outage events for calendar 2018 shows only 220 total reported events.[8] The data from NORS does not become public, nor, as far as we know, is it ever shared with the cable, satellite, phone, and so on, companies that provide the data to the FCC. The FCC states, "Given the sensitive nature of this data to both national security and commercial competitiveness, the outage data is presumed to be confidential."[9]

There are, of course, data breach reporting laws on the books today. At the end of this chapter, we will discuss why those laws have not solved the lack of information problem, but next we turn to our proposal.

A Proposal

For organizations we propose a reporting regime for computer security incidents that is closest to the DOE electrical outage reporting or, more specifically, to the first part of the DOE's mandatory two-part reporting form, OE-417.[10] The form has two parts (Schedules 1 and 2). The first part fits on two pages and is all highly structured, consisting of checkboxes, and constrained, with very short answer questions, such as "estimate number of customers affected" (excluding a short "additional comments" section). Schedule 1 is made public. Schedule 2, which asks for a narrative description, is not made public. Similarly, we envision a mandatory report that would consist of a checkbox and very short answer questions asking for the size, type, and estimated costs of a breach, along with several attributes about the organization attacked and its defenses. As mentioned, the DOE makes the Schedule 1 information from every reported electric outage incident public. We would do the same but redact the name of the organization and any geographic information. We would also round numerical reports, making them at least modestly more difficult to associate with particular incidents. The goal is not to anonymize all reports but rather to attempt to anonymize many of the reports of smaller incidents,[11] because the major incidents are often widely reported news events and may also be subject to mandatory public disclosure, so there is no point in trying to anonymize them.

Benefits

The information gathered and reported, together with an estimate of the number of organizations required to report, will give both researchers and organizations themselves the information needed to make reasonably accurate estimates of the probability of a security incident and, more specifically, the probability of a security incident of a specific cost. This is precisely the information that we have argued is needed but currently missing. It makes sense for the federal government to collect this data nationwide, but that is not absolutely necessary. If just a handful of states or even one large enough state with enough business activity were to gather and report this information, that would probably suffice. Estimates of breach probabilities based on, say, only California or only Texas would not be quite as accurate as those based on the nation as a whole, but they should still be quite good.

The collection we have in mind should be low cost for both the reporting companies and for whatever government agency collects and publishes it. There is no reason a report shouldn't fit on a two-page form, just like Schedule 1 of OE-417.

Privacy Concerns

Prior to its passage, privacy advocates "asked Congress to kill or reform the Cybersecurity Information Sharing Act, a bill that they [said hid] new government surveillance mechanisms in the guise of security protections."[12] The issue was that the shared information in CISA could include detailed information about various consumers' data or online behavior, if it was relevant to a breach. It is difficult to see how our proposal for short reporting of the size and nature of a breach and an organization's defenses could become a surveillance system in the guise of security protection. We envision businesses reporting only the size, type, and approximate cost to the business of a breach along with several relevant attributes of the business and its defenses. With a little information on which organizations are required to report, this would allow businesses and other organizations to calculate expected business losses.

THE CONSUMER RISK MANAGEMENT GOAL

Lack of relevant information is also one roadblock in the way of adequately approximating the risk management goal in the case of consumer losses, in addition to the negative externality problem. In fact, the lack of information problem is more severe for the consumer case than for the business case, as there is remarkably little research on how much data breaches cost consumers. The point a recent University of California, Berkeley study makes about distributed denial of service (DDoS) attacks applies equally to data breaches:

There is ... little research that empirically measures costs to the consumers who own the compromised devices used in cybercrimes. This lack of research makes it difficult to (1) estimate the total social cost of cyberattacks; (2) determine how costs are distributed among stakeholders; (3) make a determination about which parties are in the least cost avoider position to prevent or mitigate cyberattacks; and (4) protect and compensate consumers and third parties harmed by cyberattacks.[13]

Aggregating Consumer Cost Information

To aggregate information about the *consumer* cost of data breaches, we do *not* propose any sort of mandatory reporting by consumers to the government. It would raise significant privacy issues to require consumers to report the type of data involved in a breach, the storage location of the data, and the type and extent of the losses sustained. We propose instead government-initiated or government-funded research which focuses on consumers who consent to provide their information. The proposal is not without its problems, but we see no other effective way to ensure adequate information in the consumer case.

Providing a Legal Incentive

Even with sufficient information, profit-driven businesses lack a sufficient incentive to adequately approximate the risk management goal for consumer losses. So, why not create an incentive by imposing legal liability for losses from data breaches? There is a compelling rationale for doing so. An analogy with landlords and tenants reveals the rationale.

The "landlords" are the various kinds of businesses that store consumer data online.[14] Collectively, call them *data holders*. The "tenants" are the consumers whose data resides with the data holder. The argument is that, just as landlords can be liable for harm to tenants from unauthorized access to the landlords' buildings, so data holders should be liable for harm caused to consumers by unauthorized access to the data they store. To see why, consider a staple of the first-year Torts course in law school, the classic landlord/tenant case, *Kline v. 1500 Massachusetts*

Avenue Apartment Corporation.[15] Kline was assaulted in the common areas of the apartment building in which she lived. She sued for negligence, alleging that the building owner unreasonably failed to provide adequate security. The court agreed:

> ... where, as here, the landlord has notice of repeated criminal assaults and robberies, has notice that these crimes occurred in the portion of the premises exclusively within his control, has every reason to expect like crimes to happen again, and has the exclusive power to take preventive action, it does not seem unfair to place upon the landlord a duty to take those steps which are within his power to minimize the predictable risk to his tenants.
> ...
> As between tenant and landlord, the landlord is the only one in the position to take the necessary acts of protection required ... he is obligated to minimize the risk to his tenants. Not only as between landlord and tenant is the landlord best equipped to guard against the predictable risk of intruders, but even as between landlord and the police power of government, the landlord is in the best position to take the necessary protective measures. Municipal police cannot patrol the entryways and the hallways, the garages and the basements of private multiple unit apartment dwellings. They are neither equipped, manned, nor empowered to do so. In the area of the predictable risk which materialized in this case, only the landlord could have taken measures which might have prevented the injuries suffered by appellant.[16]

Like traditional landlords, data holders are typically in the best position to take steps to prevent the harm to the consumers whose data is being held, the *data subjects,* that may follow a data breach. So, why not require data holders to take reasonable steps to prevent harm to the data subjects?

The rationale for doing so is compelling, and, as we noted in Chapter 1, information security laws already "obligate companies to establish and maintain 'reasonable' or 'appropriate' security measures, controls, safeguards, or procedures."[17] The problem is that merely establishing laws is ineffective without a solution to the lack of information problem.

It is instructive to compare *Kline* in which the landlord can easily answer the following three questions. (1) How large is the loss from an assault in the common areas? An assault can result in significant harm—monetary, physical (including loss of life), and emotional. (2) Without additional security, what is the probability of an assault in the common areas? Quite high. The court notes that the landlord was aware of "crimes of violence, robbery, and assault which had been occurring with mounting frequency on the premises at 1500 Massachusetts Avenue."[18] (3) Are there additional investments in security that would reduce the expected loss more than the cost of the investment? The *Kline* court thought so, and it clearly thought that the landlord can determine that without precisely quantifying the harm from assault and the probability of an assault. The landlord should have realized that the expected monetary, physical, and emotional harm from assaults was significantly greater than a variety of additional monetary investments in security. The court mentions taking steps

> to guard the garage entranceways, to provide scrutiny at the main entrance of the building, to patrol the common hallways and elevators, to set up any kind of a security alarm system in the building, to provide additional locking devices on the main doors, to provide a system of announcement for authorized visitors only, to close the garage doors at appropriate hours, and to see that the entrance was manned at all times.[19]

In data breach cases, lack of relevant information means plaintiffs face insuperable difficulties in answering the relevant versions of the three questions above. The defendant will argue that its security practices were similar to the majority of other similar businesses, and the court will typically treat the defendant's conformity to the general practice as evidence that the security procedures were reasonable. Without relevant information about probabilities and losses, plaintiffs lack an adequate counter and so fail to show that the defendant's security procedures were unreasonable.[20]

There is an exception if the general practice is clearly unreasonable, but those exceptions simply underscore the plight of plaintiffs in the cases that do not fall within the exception. Consider a classic example of the exception, another staple of law school torts courses, the case of the *T.J. Hooper.*[21] In March 1928, two tugboats, the *Montrose* and the *T.J. Hooper*, encountered a gale while towing barges up the Atlantic coast, and the tugs and the barges sank. The tugs did not have shortwave radios. Had they been so equipped, they would have received reports of the storm and put in at the Delaware breakwater to ride it out in safety. Shortwave radios, however, were a new technology, and the industry standard was for tugs *not* to have one. The court nonetheless held that it was unreasonable not to equip the tug with a radio as a precaution against losses from storms. The underlying rationale is essentially the same as in *Kline*. The captain could easily answer three questions. (1) How large is the loss from a storm that sinks the tugboat and the barges? Very large. (2) What is the likelihood that a tugboat operating along the Atlantic coast will eventually encounter a major storm over the years? Very high. The expected loss then is very large. (3) Is that expected loss significantly greater than the $25 cost of the radio? Yes. So, buying the radio avoids the large expected loss, and not buying it is unreasonable.

The Wyndham breach is similar to the case of the *T.J. Hooper*. It is clear that basic precautions like firewalls would have cost less than the expected loss avoided, and Wyndham did lose in court when it challenged fines assessed by the FTC.[22] The point to emphasize is the similarity to the *T.J. Hooper*: it is easy to estimate relevant probabilities and costs. The problem is the very large number of cases in which that is not true. To see why, recall the spectrum of security investment we envisioned in Chapter 1. Egregious underinvestment lies at one end; excessive overspending at the other. The middle is home to adequate approximations of the risk management goal. An effective liability standard based on reasonableness would produce a range of plaintiff victories against data holders in the region from the egregious underspending end *up to the adequate approximation middle.* As we noted, that is not what is happening. One only sees plaintiffs winning at the egregious underspending end. The problem is lack of information about probabilities and costs as soon as one moves away from the egregious cases.

We think the best course is to discover the necessary information. That may be a long and difficult road. Some may hope for a quicker path to improving risk management. Breach notification laws may appear to be just such a road.

DATA BREACH NOTIFICATION LAWS

Are we making the issue too complicated? Won't breach notification laws allow us to achieve the consumer risk management goal? As of April 2018, every U.S. state has a breach notification law.[23] The Securities and Exchange Commission also requires companies "to inform investors about material cybersecurity risks and incidents in a timely fashion,"[24] and in the European Union the General Data Protection Regulation also requires notification. As the security expert Bruce Schneier notes, there are

> three reasons for breach notification laws. One, it's common politeness that when you lose something of someone else's, you tell him. The prevailing corporate attitude before the law—"They won't notice, and if they do notice they won't know it's us, so we are better off keeping quiet about the whole thing"—is just wrong. Two, it provides statistics to security researchers as to how pervasive the problem really is. And three, it forces companies to improve their security.[25]

We focus on the third reason. Breach notification laws certainly do lead businesses to increase security. The reason is that publicizing data breaches can impose significant costs on businesses, and the threat of such losses has led businesses to increase online security. The crucial question is: Does this increased security yield a more effective pursuit of the goal of *consumer risk management*? The answer is, at best, "Unclear."

We have found little relevant evidence, other than studies focusing on identity theft.[26] There is some evidence that breach notification laws reduce identity theft. For example, a heavily cited 2011 study found that states with data breach laws had 6.1% less identity theft.[27] One cannot simply infer, however, that an increase in security measures taken by the data holders is responsible for the reduction. Reductions in identity theft may result from a variety of factors other than increased security. Moreover, a 6.1% reduction in identity theft does not show that the consumer risk management goal has been met. After all, 6.1% is not such a large reduction. Furthermore, the harm from unauthorized access reaches far beyond identity theft. It includes harm from ransomware, viruses, denial of services attacks, and botnets engaged in fraud and other illegal activities.

Moreover, there is reason to doubt that data breach notification requirements improve consumer risk management at all. Companies' incentives under breach notification laws are to minimize the cost of compliance with those laws, not to minimize consumers' losses. Compliance costs include forensic and investigative activities, assessment and audit services, crisis team management, communications to executive management and board of directors, notification costs, remediation activities, legal expenditures, product discounts, identity protection services and regulatory interventions, and lost business. Data breach notification laws create an incentive to avoid *those* costs. It would be surprising if avoiding those *business* costs were strongly correlated with improved *consumer* risk management. Indeed, there is some reason to think that such a correlation is unlikely.

The laws define the type of event a business must report. They thus create an incentive to reduce *reportable* data breaches. They do not create an incentive to improve security in regard to problems that do not manifest themselves as reportable data breaches. As the law professor David Thaw notes, specific statutory regulations like data breach notification laws can drive "perhaps-otherwise-sufficient security budgets toward specific compliance objectives such as encryption. This, in turn, reduces the available resources for other security activities, and forces CISOs to focus on meeting minimum compliance objectives rather than prioritizing the greatest threats they feel their organization faces."[28]

CONCLUSION

Data breach notification laws are an uncertain road to the business and consumer risk management goals. The more certain, if longer, road to improving consumer risk management includes reporting to get the necessary information about the cost and probability of breaches. Reporting should be mandatory for businesses but voluntary for consumers (because of privacy concerns). To meet the consumer risk management goal, legal liability is necessary to overcome the negative externality problem. We have proposed a combination of negligence liability and (in Chapter 3) FTC actions.

Now suppose sufficient information about relevant costs and probabilities is readily available. Who is best able to effectively and efficiently use that information to mount an appropriate defense? In the next chapter, we argue that the task of defense may in many cases be outsourced to defensive experts.

ENDNOTES

1. See, e.g., "Underinvesting in Cybersecurity: How Do You Know How Much Security Is Enough?" 2014, http://www.symantec.com/connect/blogs/underinvesting-cybersecurity-how-do-you-know-how-much-security-enough.
2. "Disrupt and Grow: U.S. CEO Outlook for 2017," KMPG, 2017, https://www.msspalert.com/cybersecurity-research/kpmg-us-ceo-cybersecurity-survey-findings/.

3. PricewaterhouseCoopers, "Strengthening Digital Society against Cyber Shocks: Key Findings from the Global State of Information Security Survey 2018," 2018, https://www.pwc.com/us/en/services/consulting/cybersecurity/library/information-security-survey/strengthening-digital-society-against-cyber-shocks.html.

4. Some worry that the data may have limited predictive value: "Because cyber risk is both growing and rapidly evolving, information about the past may be of limited predictive value." A. G. Baribeau, "Cyber Insurance: The Actuarial Conundrum," *Insurance Communicators* 33, August 2015.

5. "Cybersecurity Information Sharing Act of 2105," Emails and Newsletters, 2015, https://www.cisecurity.org/newsletter/cybersecurity-information-sharing-act-of-2015/.

6. 15 U.S. Code § 772 mandates the sharing of the information. Emily Fisher, Joseph H. Eto, and Kristina Hamachi LaCommare, "Understanding Bulk Power Reliability: The Importance of Good Data and A Critical Review of Existing Sources," in *45th Hawaii International Conference on System Science (HICSS)* (IEEE, 2012), 2159–2168, http://ieeexplore.ieee.org/abstract/document/6149274/.

7. Federal Communications Commission, "Network Outage Reporting System (NORS)," December 3, 2015, https://www.fcc.gov/network-outage-reporting-system-nors.

8. Department of Energy, "Electric Disturbance Events (OE-417) Annual Summaries," accessed February 17, 2019, https://www.oe.netl.doe.gov/OE417_annual_summary.aspx.

9. Federal Communications Commission, "Network Outage Reporting System (NORS)."

10. Department of Energy, "ISER—Electric Disturbance Events (OE-417)," accessed February 17, 2019, https://www.oe.netl.doe.gov/oe417.aspx.

11. We write "attempt to anonymize" rather than "anonymize" because of the frequent successes of computer scientists in deanonymizing supposedly anonymized datasets over the past decade or two. See, e.g., A. Narayanan and V. Shmatikov, "Robust De-Anonymization of Large Sparse Datasets," in *Proceedings of the IEEE Symposium on Security and Privacy*, 2008, 111–125; A. Narayanan and V. Shmatikov, "De-Anonymizing Social Networks," in *Proceedings of the IEEE Symposium on Security and Privacy*, 2009, 173–187; P. Ohm, "Broken Promises of Privacy: Responding to the Surprising Failure of Anonymization," *UCLA Law Review* 57 (2010): 1701–77.

12. Wired Staff, "CISA Security Bill Passes Senate with Privacy Flaws Unfixed," *Wired*, October 27, 2015, https://www.wired.com/2015/10/cisa-cybersecurity-information-sharing-act-passes-senate-vote-with-privacy-flaws/.

13. K. Fong, R. Raghavan, and P. Rowland, "rIoT | Quantifying Consumer Harms," UC Berkeley School of Information, 2018, https://www.ischool.berkeley.edu/projects/2018/riot-quantifying-consumer-harms.

14. Businesses range from resource- and expertise-rich corporations to mom-and-pop retailers. There is a pressing question of how small and medium-sized businesses are to meet the risk management goals we suggest here.

15. *Kline v. 1500 Massachusetts Ave. Apartment Corp.*, F.2d 477 (Court of Appeals, District of Columbia 1970).

16. *Kline v. 1500 Massachusetts Ave. Apartment Corp.*, F.2d at 484.

17. T. J. Smedinghoff, "Defining the Legal Standard for Information Security: What Does 'Reasonable' Security Really Mean?" in *Securing Privacy in the Internet Age*, eds. Gelman, L., and Radin M. J. (Stanford University Press, 2008), 19–40.

18. *Kline v. 1500 Massachusetts Ave. Apartment Corp.*, F.2d at 480.

19. *Kline v. 1500 Massachusetts Ave. Apartment Corp.*, F.2d at 480.

20. Note that three questions concern amounts of harm and probabilities of harm in general, not just in the case of this or that plaintiff. Courts are currently split on whether a plaintiff who has not yet suffered a concrete harm (as opposed to the conjecture of a future harm) can sue the business that was breached, but if those cases are allowed to go forward, the three questions about harms and probabilities arise there too.

21. The *T.J. Hooper*, 60 F. 2d 737 (Circuit Court of Appeals, 2nd Circuit 1932).

22. To avoid any confusion, we should note that Wyndham was the plaintiff in *FTC v. Wyndham*. The events leading to the case began when the FTC opened an investigation of Wyndham's security practices. FTC investigations typically end with the FTC and the business reaching an agreement about how the business will change and improve its business practices. When the business fails to come to terms with the FTC, it may challenge the FTC's rulings against it in court.

23. Government Relations and Policy at Van Ness Feldman, "Critical Infrastructure: 2018 Cybersecurity Year in Review/2019 Year Ahead Analysis," *National Law Review*, January 24, 2019, https://

www.natlawreview.com/article/critical-infrastructure-2018-cybersecurity-year-review2019-year-ahead-analysis.

24. Securities and Exchange Commission, "Commission Statement and Guidance on Public Company Cybersecurity Disclosures," n.d., https://www.sec.gov/rules/interp/2018/33-10459.pdf. The 2018 statement reiterated its 2011 warning that investors needed to be informed of data breaches. The 2018 statement was motivated by the rash of data breaches, including the massive 2013 Yahoo breach which affected Yahoo's three billion account holders.

25. B. Schneier, "State Data Breach Notification Laws: Have They Helped?" *Schneier on Security* (blog), January 2009, https://www.schneier.com/essays/archives/2009/01/state_data_breach_no.html.

26. D. Thaw's work is an important exception. Thaw argues that "an affirmative presumption of notification is superior from a cybersecurity perspective. Such a presumption avoids disincentivizing thorough cybersecurity investigations, which are one of the most important tools in protecting consumers against future data breaches and securing existing information systems." D. Thaw, "Data Breach (Regulatory) Effects," *Cardozo Law Review de Novo* 2015 (2015): 151–64.

27. S. Romanosky, R. Telang, and A. Acquisti, "Do Data Breach Disclosure Laws Reduce Identity Theft?" *Journal of Policy Analysis and Management* 30, no. 2 (March 1, 2011): 256–86, https://doi.org/10.1002/pam.20567.

28. D. Thaw, "The Efficacy of Cybersecurity Regulation," *Georgia State University Law Review* 30, 2014: 368.

CHAPTER 5

Outsourcing Security

THE LAST CHAPTER ARGUED for centralizing the collection of information relevant to data breach defense. This chapter argues for centralizing the defensive measures themselves by outsourcing them to specialists—managed security service providers (MSSPs) as they are now typically called. One good reason for discussing MSSPs is that they are an increasingly popular solution to network security, and, as we argue in the next chapter, they will be essential in providing adequate security on the Internet of Things (IoT). Another reason for discussing MSSPs is that the improved security they offer comes at a price. Depending on what services they provide, a massive amount of information can flow through MSSPs. This makes the MSSPs themselves an attractive target for data breaches. Additionally, MSSPs also shift who controls security defenses, which raises privacy concerns. The massive amount of data that can flow through an MSSP creates opportunities for MSSPs to monetize customer data for business purposes and also centralizes the data for potential governmental surveillance. As with most outsourcing of specialty services, a key benefit is that the service, in this case security service, will be provided by an entity with greater expertise, and the MSSP and its client may use contracts to reallocate between themselves liability the law may impose on either of them.

THE RISE OF MANAGED SECURITY SERVICE PROVIDERS (MSSPs)

A large number of companies offer a wide variety of MSSP services. A small sample: AT&T, IBM, and Verizon have divisions that are MSSPs, and FireEye, Paladion, and Trustwave are primarily MSSPs. Currently, the most popular services to outsource are security monitoring, security testing, security evaluation of third parties, security training, and incident response.[1] However, a very wide range of services are offered. For example, IBM's Managed Security Services advertises on their website that they can provide: "Firewall management, Information event management, Intelligent log management on cloud, Intrusion detection and prevention system management, Security intelligence analyst, Security-rich web gateway management, Unified threat management, Secure SD-WAN, IBM X-Force Cloud Security Services, Endpoint security services, and Amazon GuardDuty services."[2] For our purposes, however, we can for the most part simply talk of managed security without distinguishing types of service.

Managed security services are a relatively recent development. It is still largely true that each end user individually manages the user's defense against unauthorized access. By "end users," we mean those who more or less control their own computers, and who—unlike ISPs and content delivery networks—do not mediate Internet connectivity to any significant extent.[3] End users are a diverse group that includes businesses of all sizes, a variety of organizations, and home users, although the true MSSPs currently are not targeting home users. This decentralized status quo in which end users are the first line of defense is a consequence of the influence of the *end-to-end principle*.

The end-to-end principle dates back to the early days of the Internet and states that services that could conceivably be placed either at computers at the endpoints of the Internet or somewhere in the middle of the networks making up the Internet should be located at the endpoints, the computers. Hence, security services are on end user computers and endpoint local networks. There is general agreement that adherence to the end-to-end principle "dramatically expanded the uses to which data networks could be put and triggered the explosive growth of the Internet"[4] from its genesis as a 1960s government project into the 2000s.

Outsourcing security departs from the end-to-end principle by moving defensive measures away from the end user periphery.

ARGUMENTS FOR OUTSOURCING

There are two arguments for outsourcing security. The first is that it provides more efficient defense; the second, is that it provides more effective defense.

More Efficient Defense

In a significant number of cases, outsourcing security is more efficient than providing one's own defense. An analogy with health care shows why.[5] Divide health care into the detection of diseases and their treatment (including the development of treatments and preventive measures), on the one hand, and day-to-day health maintenance on the other. Doctor offices, hospitals, and other care facilities centralize detection. Until recently, day-to-day health maintenance has fallen mainly to individuals. Health care apps may change that. They decentralize information collection, but still feed the information to entities specializing in the analysis of the information—doctors, hospitals, and other entities.[6]

Imagine we handled health care the way we currently handle computer and network defense. Each "end user"—each person (or perhaps group, organization, business)—would hire a health care team (of one or more people) to provide care *exclusively* to that user. End users would incur the high costs of hiring a full-time health care team, but, apart from day-to-day health maintenance, the team would be mostly idle. Most people for most of their lives do not get ill very often. In addition, people would suffer from new diseases that would either go undetected or have no treatment. The detection of new diseases and the development of treatments for them requires centralized information collection and analysis.[7] This would be a massively inefficient way to deliver health care. The same is true of computer and network security. Bruce Schneier emphasizes the point: "Vigilant monitoring means keeping up to date on new vulnerabilities, new hacker tools, new security products, and new software releases. Outsourced security companies can spread these costs across all customers."[8]

Providing adequate security can be prohibitively expensive for small and medium-sized businesses, so outsourcing is an increasingly popular solution. "In a recent survey of 287 U.S.-based IT and business professionals … , 56 percent of the respondents said that their [small and medium sized] organizations are enlisting outside consultants to help with information security strategy, and 40% said they're turning to MSSPs."[9]

The efficiency argument for MSSPs applies most forcefully to medium and small organizations. However, even though a large business may have the resources to provide effective defense on its own, an MSSP may still offer significant cost savings. Outsourcing security has, for example, increased significantly in the financial sector. The European Banking Authority notes that

> Over recent years, there has been an increasing interest of financial institutions to outsource business activities in order to reduce costs and improve their flexibility and efficiency. In a context of digitalisation and increasing importance of new financial technology (fintech) providers, financial institutions are adapting their business models to embrace such technologies. Some have increased the use of fintech solutions and have launched respective projects to improve their cost efficiency as the intermediation margins from the traditional banking business model are put under pressure by the low interest rate environment. Outsourcing is a way to get relatively easy access to new technologies and to achieve economies of scale.[10]

Better Defense

MSSPs offer a potential *information* advantage in addition to the efficiency advantage. Each business customer of an MSSP benefits because the MSSP's *other* customers provide the MSSP with access to information about attacks that the business does not have. For the MSSP, "network attacks are everyday occurrences; its experts know exactly how to respond to any given attack, because in all likelihood they have already seen it many times before."[11]

In addition, outsourcers increasingly offer machine learning and AI approaches to threat detection, and those approaches typically lie outside the expertise of even many large businesses. Threat detection is in part a matter of identifying relevant patterns in network traffic, and machine learning and AI excel at the pattern recognition task.

MONITORING, MONETIZING, AND PRIVACY

Real-time threat detection requires that the MSSP monitor the data flowing in and out of a business. The MSSP Cipher, for example, offers security monitoring in two forms: Fully-Managed Security Services, and Co-Managed Security Services.[12] In the fully managed service, "the managed security services provider (MSSP) will extend its tools and technologies to your organization and monitor and manage them on a 24 × 7 × 365 basis."[13] The co-managed service appeals to those who "own an array of security devices but remain short on internal security resources required to manage these solutions on a 24 × 7 × 365 basis ... This model allows your staff to focus on other strategic security projects and helps offload the intensive job of monitoring and managing security events."[14] A recent report on the use of MSSPs in retailing notes that "90% of respondents are leaning on managed security service providers to provide event monitoring for IT infrastructure logs, firewalls and intrusion detection systems (IDS)/intrusion prevention systems (IPS)."[15] The report's explanation is that "[d]ue to increasing cost concerns and challenges faced with in-house talent, participating organizations are looking to outsource the security functions to an MSSP instead of building the capability in house for monitoring events from IT infrastructure logs, firewalls, and IDS/IPS, as well as to conduct penetration tests."[16] In short, the MSSPs are monitoring the flow of data into and out of their clients' organizations on a continuous basis.

Monitoring the flow of data creates a lucrative business opportunity for MSSPs. They can analyze the information and sell analyses to third parties, and they can also sell access to the data itself. Doing so reduces the informational privacy of the subjects of the data. Informational privacy is the ability to determine for yourself when others may collect and how they may use your information.[17] Businesses significantly reduce that ability when they decide how your information is used. How many outsourcing companies monetize data? The question is difficult to answer since contracts between an MSSP and its business clients are typically not publicly available. As a second best, we reviewed privacy policies on outsourcing companies' websites to assess their attitudes in that context toward monetizing information. A few policies say the company transfers personal information to third parties. Some assert that the company does not transfer personal information to third parties for those third parties' marketing purposes while other policies note that the company transfers information to partners and affiliates.

A CHANGING LANDSCAPE

The rise of MSSPs changes the data breach landscape. For one thing, MSSPs are now a target. "Hackers are attacking MSSPs, MSPs and CSPs as the weak link in a supply chain to get to their customers."[18] For another, the relationship between an MSSP and its client is contractual. The contract allocates the risk of loss and liability in the case of a data breach, and it also defines what the MSSP may do with the information to which it has access. With MSSPs in the picture, the study of defenses against data breaches becomes a study of MSSP defenses *and* a study of contractual allocations of risk and liability. These issues merit more investigation, but we put them aside and turn instead to the IoT. Adequate defense against data breaches on the IoT will almost certainly require outsourcing security to MSSPs, and, in that context, MSSPs will have a strong incentive to monetize data.

ENDNOTES

1. C. Terrill, "The Top 5 Security Functions to Outsource," *Forbes*, March 13, 2017, https://www.forbes.com/sites/christieterrill/2017/03/13/the-top-5-security-functions-to-outsource/. For a similar summary from 2016, see B. Stackpole, "Why (and When) Outsourcing Security Makes Sense," *CIO*, September 21, 2016, https://www.cio.com/article/3120650/security/why-and-when-outsourcing-security-makes-sense.html.
2. "Managed Security Services," IBM, November 23, 2018, https://www.ibm.com/security/services/managed-security-services.
3. Users connected in peer-to-peer networks do not fit comfortably into this definition. They control their own computers in the way residential users, for example, typically do, but they also mediate Internet connectivity. We can put this complication aside for our purposes.
4. J. E. Nuechterlein and P. J. Weiser, *Digital Crossroads: American Telecommunications Policy in the Internet Age* (MIT Press, 2005), 43.
5. B. Schneier, "The Case for Outsourcing Security," *Computer* 35, no. 4, April 2002: supl20–21, https://doi.org/10.1109/MC.2002.1012426.
6. L. Andrews, "Privacy Policies of Android Diabetes Apps and Sharing of Health Information," *JAMA: Journal of the American Medical Association* 315, 2016: 1051.
7. A. L. Fairchild et al., *Searching Eyes: Privacy, the State, and Disease Surveillance in America* (Berkeley: University of California Press, 2007).
8. B. Schneier, "The Case for Outsourcing Security."
9. Stackpole, "Why (and When) Outsourcing Security Makes Sense."
10. "Consultation Paper: EBA Draft Guidelines on Outsourcing Arrangements," European Banking Authority, June 22, 2018, https://www.eba.europa.eu/documents/10180/2260326/Consultation+Paper+on+draft+Guidelines+on+outsourcing+arrangements+%28EBA-CP-2018-11%29.pdf.
11. B. Schneier, "The Case for Outsourcing Security."

12. "Managed Security Services," Cipher, accessed January 7, 2019, https://cipher.com/managed-security-services/.
13. "Managed Security Services."
14. "Managed Security Services."
15. D. Kobialka, "MSSP Benchmark Survey: 90% of Retailers Use Event Monitoring Services," MSSP Alert, August 22, 2018, https://www.msspalert.com/cybersecurity-research/retailers-outsourcing-trends/.
16. Retail Cyber Intelligence Sharing Center (R-CISC), "2018 Managed Security Service Provider (MSSP): Benchmark Survey," 2018, https://r-cisc.org/wp-content/uploads/MSSP-White-Paper_8-21-18.pdf.
17. A. Westin, *Privacy and Freedom* (New York: Atheneum Press, 1967), 7.
18. D. H. Kass, "DHS Memo: Hackers Exploiting MSPs to Attack Customers' Networks," MSSP Alert, October 3, 2018, https://www.msspalert.com/cybersecurity-news/dhs-warning-msps-csps/. The DHS memo (Department of Homeland Security, "Alert (TA18-276B): Advanced Persistent Threat Activity Exploiting Managed Service Providers," October 3, 2018, https://www.us-cert.gov/ncas/alerts/TA18-276B.) refers only to Managed Service Providers (MSPs) not MSSPs, but MSSPs are MSPs specializing in security, and their access to client data makes them attractive targets.

CHAPTER 6

The Internet of Things

Ellen and Nathan Rigney had a Nest baby monitor in their bedroom linked to a Nest camera in their baby's room.[1] One night they heard expletives over the monitor followed by "I'm going to kidnap your baby" and "I'm in your baby's room." The baby was sound asleep and alone. Their Internet-connected Nest camera had been hacked. This is a particularly appalling example of the increasingly common horror stories about Internet of Things (IoT) hacking, albeit not one connected to data breaches in the narrow sense in which we have been using the term. In this chapter, however, we use the term *data breach* in the broad sense we noted in Chapter 1. Data breaches in this sense include not only breaches of confidentiality but also breaches of integrity and availability. The broader use applies the label to events that exploit, corrupt, destroy, or block access to information. Data breaches then include denial of service attacks, ransomware attacks, and destructive hacking that corrupts or destroys data. This broader understanding of data breaches is useful in assessing the threats that the IoT poses.

We begin by defining the IoT.

WHAT IS THE IoT?

An IoT is any network that connects "things" to the Internet. When we refer to *the* IoT, we mean the totality of all IoTs. The "things" can be anything, but the term typically indicates a focus on items that were unconnected until relatively recently—cars, thermostats, kitchen appliances, wearables, medical devices, drones, baby monitors, factory robotic systems, and so on. To count as connected, a thing must be able to communicate with the Internet. Optional capabilities include sensing, capturing, storing, and processing data and effecting changes in the things in a physical or virtual environment. A 2017 Gartner estimate puts the number of IoT-connected devices at 8.4 billion worldwide and projects 20.4 billion by 2020.[2] For our purposes, it is sufficient to consider the "things" as being connected to the network and containing sensors, actuators, or both and sometimes also data storage and analysis (the same device may be one or more of these). Billions of sensors collect data and feed it to the data storage and analysis components. Those components instruct actuators to take actions (control air-conditioning and heating, steer cars, and so on).

Our concern is with data breaches of those components. Lack of adequate security on the IoT increases the likelihood of such breaches. We focus on four significant reasons for inadequate IoT security: the structure of the IoT, market pressures, manufacturer inexperience, and consumer inaction.

THREE IoT SECURITY ISSUES

IoT Structure

As we noted in Chapter 3, complexity is the enemy of security, and the IoT has a very complex structure. Billions of sensors and actuators create a huge attack surface for hackers. Those sensors and actuators communicate with data storage and analysis components through gateways. The protocols of the sensors and actuators often need to be translated into another format. "The different ways of fusing such protocols can have enormous security implications, potentially introducing new attack surfaces into an enterprise."[3] The combination of the vast number of IoT things plus all those different protocols equals tremendous complexity.

In addition, as Bruce Schneier notes in his discussion of the IoT, "[i]n order for companies to control us in the ways they want, they will build systems that allow for remote control ... This is a design requirement that runs counter to good security, because it gives outside attackers an avenue to gain access."[4] Samsung provides an example. When touting its ability to manage mobile devices, it notes, on a web page entitled "The Next Mobile Economy" that "[m]obile empowerment can't come at the expense of fleet control, so we balance the work tech that employees expect with the ability to easily control devices remotely."[5] The result is a very broad attack surface. The attacker needs to find one vulnerability in this broad front. The defender's task, on the other hand, is to secure the entire attack surface. The IoT structure can make the attacker's task much easier, and the defender's much harder.

Market Pressures

The profit-maximizing strategy is to produce low-cost, easy-to-operate devices. Devices typically lack any significant protection against unauthorized access as that would increase costs and could reduce ease of use. Devices may not even be patchable when vulnerabilities are discovered, or may be difficult to patch.

Manufacturer Inexperience

Cybersecurity is a new concern for many of the industries involved in the IoT, and many companies lack relevant security experience. The situation is similar to the early days of the Internet when businesses and governments rushed to embrace the Internet without much thought about or experience with security. The IoT has created a new Internet "gold rush" with many of the "miners" paying insufficient attention to security issues. Older, unpatched operating systems are a serious problem as the *Harvard Business Review* notes, IoT "devices are often manufactured in millions, are very likely to have a much older embedded operating system which is likely not patched."[6]

Consumer Inaction

The owners of IoT devices may not especially care about securing them. They often, for example, do not change default passwords.[7] As Bruce Schneier notes, with regard to hacked webcams and DVR uses in denial of service attacks, "The owners … don't care. Their devices were cheap to buy, they still work, and they don't know any of the victims of the attacks."[8] This is not the case of the large corporation with a critical component of its business such as its POS. Rather, this is a camera, DVR, or router in somebody's home. Often, if that device is successfully attacked, it will still work for its owner most or almost all of the time, while it *also* serves as a component of an attack on some third party.

RECENT ATTACKS

Recent attacks involving the IoT illustrate the current lack of security. It is convenient to classify the attacks using the CIA triad—confidentiality, integrity, authenticity.

Attacks on Confidentiality

Attacks on confidentiality involving the IoT will often create data breaches in the sense we have discussed in earlier chapters. First, we give an example of a data breach whose only connection to the IoT is that the data that was stolen happened to be originally collected via IoT devices. Then we will give an example of an attack on stored data accomplished at least in part by compromising an IoT device.

MyFitnessPal

MyFitnessPal from sports gear and apparel company Under Armour is an iPhone and Android app that tracks diet and exercise. In February 2018, a data breach of the Under Armour servers gave hackers access to up to 150 million user accounts containing usernames, email addresses, and hashed passwords.[9] Under Armour has not yet disclosed the cause of the breach, but it evidently did not involve compromising the app itself, though it did give the hackers access to information collected from the app. How common are data breaches involving access to IoT-collected information? We have not been able to find studies answering precisely that question, but the large number of health care data breaches makes it reasonable to assume they are common. The first eight months of 2018 saw 229 health care data breaches.[10] Given the widespread and increasing use of Internet-connected health care devices and health care apps, it is reasonable to suppose that some of these breaches involved at least potential access to IoT-collected information.

The Internet-Connected Fish Tank

In 2017, hackers downloaded an unnamed casino's high-roller list after penetrating the casino's network though the Internet-connected fish tank in the casino's lobby.[11] The rationale for the connection was convenience. The casino could remotely monitor the tank in order to feed the fish and adjust salinity and temperature.[12]

The fish tank attack is the only example our research revealed of a compromised IoT device leading to a data breach (as opposed to a DDoS or ransomware attack). There may, of course, be others that have gone unnoticed or unreported. In any case, many predict such data breaches in the future. "Well over three-quarters ... of professionals ... in corporate governance or risk oversight say that a serious data breach caused by an unsecured IoT device is likely to occur in their business in the next two years [by 2020]."[13]

Attacks on Integrity

Our research has not revealed attacks on integrity. The IoT nonetheless raises significant concerns about attacks on integrity. The IoT's current lack of security exposes information to attacks that alter it. Those attacks can change the effects that the IoT's actuators produce. As one commentator put it, "There is a fundamental difference between crashing your computer and losing your spreadsheet data, and crashing your pacemaker and losing your life."[14]

Attacks on Availability

Hackers use compromised IoT devices in distributed denial of service (DDoS) and ransomware attacks. One well-known example is the 2016 DDoS attack that brought down KrebsOnSecurity.com, the website of the investigative journalist Brian Krebs. The motive was likely retaliation for Krebs cybercrime investigative reporting. The attack was launched from a botnet of 24,000 security cameras, DVRs, and routers. Hackers installed Mirai malware on the devices by exploiting the fact that users frequently do not change default passwords. They scanned for open Telnet ports, and, when they found one, they tried 61 username/password combinations often used as defaults.

AN EVEN STRONGER CASE FOR OUTSOURCING

The efficiency and effectiveness arguments for outsourcing security are even stronger in the case of the IoT. Efficiency: The sensors and actuators are spread over all types of users: residential and businesses and organizations of all sizes. If it is inefficient for individual organizations to each protect themselves against unauthorized access at the end points of the traditional Internet, it is even more so to spread that protection widely across billions of sensors and actuators. Effectiveness: The IoT adds a significant layer of complexity to the traditional Internet. If outsourcing security provides more effective defense in that case to an end user, it is even more likely to do so in the case of the IoT.

THE MOTIVE TO MONETIZE INFORMATION

The IoT will generate massive amounts of data. Much of it may flow through security outsourcing companies. That data has enormous economic value as an input to analyses that support marketing, advertising, business planning, and product development.[15] That means that outsourcing companies have two potential sources of revenue: fees for providing security, and revenue generated as a supplier and/or analyzer of data.

Will outsourcing companies embrace the second option? It may seem so. Revenue from supplying or analyzing data could allow a company to lower what it charges for security services, and would appear to make them more competitive. Between two outsourcing companies offering equivalent security services, why wouldn't businesses choose the less expensive one? They will—unless they prefer to pay a higher price to exclude their information from exploitation by their outsourcing company. The market of businesses that outsource their security is likely to segment into businesses opting for a lower price in exchange for their data and those willing to pay a higher price to protect their data. The second group would likely include businesses that are themselves generating revenue by supplying or analyzing data.

There is one entity that will almost certainly outsource security and allow its outsourcing company to generate revenue from its data: smart cities. A city makes itself "smart" by linking a variety of activities to the Internet in order to improve the quality of those activities and decrease the cost of providing them. Typical examples of linked activities include transportation, parking, lighting, utilities, surveillance, and maintenance of public areas, public safety, firefighting, and law enforcement. Linking these activities to the Internet involves an extensive use of the IoT.

One way to provide that infrastructure is to outsource the task. The City of San Mateo in California, for example, uses Streetline to provide "smart" parking. Streetline's proposal to the city makes it clear that they provide infrastructure in exchange for the city's participation in a "partnership program involving advertising and sponsorship." The proposal describes a system of sensors that would provide "real-time parking information for every on- and off-street public space."[16] Streetline proposes to fund software, hardware, and implementation in exchange for the city's participation "in a partnership program involving advertising and sponsorship as part of the City's downtown parking program."[17]

ENDNOTES

1. A. B. Wang, "'I'm in Your Baby's Room': A Hacker Took over a Baby Monitor and Broadcast Threats, Parents Say," *Washington Post*, December 20, 2018, https://www.washingtonpost.com/technology/2018/12/20/nest-cam-baby-monitor-hacked-kidnap-threat-came-device-parents-say/.
2. "Gartner Says 8.4 Billion Connected 'Things' Will Be in Use in 2017, Up 31 Percent from 2016," Gartner, n.d., https://www.gartner.com/en/newsroom/press-releases/2017-02-07-gartner-says-8-billion-connected-things-will-be-in-use-in-2017-up-31-percent-from-2016.
3. B. Russell and D. Van Duren, *Practical Internet of Things Security* (Birmingham, UK: Packt Publishing/ebooks Account, 2016).
4. B. Schneier, *Click Here to Kill Everybody: Security and Survival in a Hyper-Connected World* (New York: W. W. Norton & Company, 2018), 64.
5. "Next Mobile Economy," Samsung Electronics America, accessed November 13, 2018, https://www.samsung.com/us/business/solutions/topics/next-mobile-economy/.
6. M. E. Porter and J. E. Heppelmann, "How Smart, Connected Products Are Transforming Competition," *Harvard Business Review*, November 1, 2014, https://hbr.org/2014/11/how-smart-connected-products-are-transforming-competition.
7. Porter and Heppelmann.
8. B. Schneier, "We Need to Save the Internet from the Internet of Things—Schneier on Security," *Schneier on Security* (blog), October 6, 2016, https://www.schneier.com/essays/archives/2016/10/we_need_to_save_the_html.
9. C. Bonnington, "The MyFitnessPal Hack Affects 150 Million Users. It Could've Been Even Worse.," *Slate Magazine*, accessed September 8, 2018, https://slate.com/technology/2018/03/myfitnesspal-hack-under-armour-data-breach.html.
10. J. Spizer, "6.1 M Healthcare Data Breach Victims in 2018: 5 of the Biggest Breaches So Far," Becker's Health IT & CIO Report, August 22, 2018, https://www.beckershospitalreview.com/cybersecurity/6-1m-healthcare-data-breach-victims-in-2018-5-of-the-biggest-breaches-so-far.html.

11. O. Williams-Grut, "Hackers Once Stole a Casino's High-Roller Database through a Thermometer in the Lobby Fish Tank," Business Insider, n.d., https://www.businessinsider.com/hackers-stole-a-casinos-database-through-a-thermometer-in-the-lobby-fish-tank-2018-4.
12. L. Mathews, "Criminals Hacked a Fish Tank to Steal Data from a Casino," *Forbes*, July 27, 2017, https://www.forbes.com/sites/leemathews/2017/07/27/criminals-hacked-a-fish-tank-to-steal-data-from-a-casino/.
13. S. Shah, "Serious IoT Data Breach Likely by 2020, Say Risk Professionals," *Internet of Business* (blog), March 26, 2018, https://internetofbusiness.com/iot-data-breach-third-party/.
14. Schneier, *Click Here to Kill Everybody*, 82.
15. Porter and Heppelmann, "How Smart, Connected Products Are Transforming Competition."
16. "Administrative Report," 2014, https://docplayer.net/62673985-Administrative-report.html.
17. "Administrative Report."

Human Vulnerabilities

T HE TOP HUMAN VULNERABILITY hackers exploit is the human propensity to trust. Recall the vampire movie analogy we gave in Chapter 1. Vampires can't enter a house unless invited in, but of course in a vampire movie some innocent, ignorant person does just that. Far too many invite hackers into their computers and networks by, for example, clicking on malicious attachments from unknown senders and succumbing to phishing.

PHISHING

Phishing is the use of an electronic communication, most often email, that masquerades as being from someone trustworthy to induce the recipient to reveal information such as usernames and passwords. It has been extremely widespread and successful in recent years. For example, in a case study entitled, "Examining how a China-based threat actor stole vast amounts of PII," Mandiant notes that phishing attacks have been a theme year after year, the China-based attack being yet another example: "It began with … enticing a user to follow a malicious link in a phishing email. The link downloaded a backdoor. Once the threat actor obtained a foothold, the … [attack moved on to] the identification of databases with the greatest volume of PII."[1] That case study was from Mandiant's 2016 annual report on security trends. Not much has changed since. Mandiant's 2018 report states, "Phishing continues to be a primary preferred method of compromising organizations because of its simplicity and effectiveness."[2]

Email phishing has played a role in many data breaches, not just the anonymous one described in Mandiant's case study. We saw in Chapter 1 that a successful email phish of the contractor Fazio was the first step in the Target breach. It was the first step in a successful 2011 attack on RSA, which was notable because RSA is a top security firm providing security to organizations such as defense contractors.

Phishing is by no means the only way hackers masquerade as someone else to exploit people's trust. Other examples include various other forms of social engineering. The term *social engineering* means using deception to manipulate someone into revealing information or doing something such as clicking on a link in an email that will eventually reveal information or install malware or the like. Social engineering also refers more generally to the social science that studies how to influence en masse the attitudes and behavior of large groups. The Dutch industrialist, C. Van Marken, coined the term in that sense in 1894.[3] In the Internet context, it refers more specifically to pretending to be someone else in order to gain access to a computer or network, or, more generally, to obtain any confidential information. Social engineering in that sense is not confined to the Internet. Skip tracers (professionals specializing in locating people) have practiced social engineering for years, and so have debt collectors, bounty hunters, private investigators, journalists, and perpetrators of frauds of all sorts.

Within the Internet context, emails are the most common vector for social engineering, particularly social engineering, which is an early step in a data breach. An email may have an attachment that launches malware (e.g., the phishing email to Fazio in the Target breach), or links that will cause something bad to happen if clicked upon, or a request for a reply containing information.

However, there are other forms of social engineering. First, there is plain old *pretexting:* the criminal calls via phone, or even shows up in person, telling some false story about why they need information. For example, a hacker impersonates somebody from an organization's tech support team, and explains why they need a person's username and password. Another form of social engineering is "shoulder surfing": hanging out someplace such as a coffee shop or food court very close to the targeted organization and trying to see somebody's typing on a laptop or smartphone as they enter a username and password.

For our purposes, it is convenient to distinguish two ways in which social engineering creates vulnerabilities.[4] We use the distinction later in proposing a solution to phishing. The first way is the "attractive offer." A good example is Hewlett-Packard's video starring Christian Slater as a hacker whose malware targets unsecured printers. Slater penetrates an office in which an employee Janice is having a birthday. Standing (presumably as the unseen malware) by Janice's computer as she receives an email, Slater narrates: "Gift certificate from your favorite spa to honor the big day? How thoughtful! Now all you got to do is print it. Come on Janice. It's legit. … We all know you love a good foot rub. You just got to print it out. [As Janice's prints,] That's it."[5] When Janice prints, she installs malware on the office network. The offer of the spa gift certificate is perhaps too good to be true, and in any event the spa should be sending the gift certificate to Janice's personal email, not to her work email, as Janice would realize on reflection. But she does not reflect. She takes the bait of the attractive offer.

The second way in which social engineering exploits trust is by presenting misleading information. In some uses of highly targeted phishing emails—known as *spear phishing*—hackers create the illusion of authenticity. They typically study their targets in advance in order to include genuine employee names and titles in emails that appear to originate from an appropriate sender. The tone and timing of the email may also reflect workplace culture. The email asks the recipient to carry out some typical task. Misled by the appearance of authenticity, the recipient does as requested and thereby unwittingly installs malware. One may object that Janice's email with the spa offer is in this category. It contains genuine information designed to mislead her. The hacker knew her birthday and the name of her favorite spa. The difference is that the email did not ask Janice to carry out some function that she would normally do from her work email. The key component was the attractive offer. This is not to say that the attractive offer/misleading information distinction is a sharp one. Far from it. There are any number of intermediate cases. For example, in 2004, West Point, as part of a security exercise, sent emails to over 500 cadets from a fictitious colonel instructing the cadets to click on a particular link to clear up a problem with their grades. Over 80% of the cadets did so.[6] (They arrived at a website informing them that they had been successfully lured.) Did the email include an attractive offer to clear up a grade problem? Or should it be seen as a relatively routine academic activity presented with apparent authenticity? The distinction is far from sharp, but that does not matter for the use we make of it in the next section.

EDUCATION AND TRAINING

Hackers exploit the human propensity to trust, so the solution is to make people appropriately less trusting. This is where the attractive offer/misleading information distinction is helpful.

Attractive Offers

It makes good sense to educate and train people to reflect before they act so that they do not take the hackers' attractive offers bait. Learning to recognize unsafe Internet situations is part of learning to live in the Internet world. "Learning to live in the world" instruction is a standard part of the instruction of children. We teach them how to cross a street ("Look left, look right, look left again"[7]), and we teach them a great deal more—including not to accept the attractive candy from strangers. It is no wonder that we need education and instruction about how to live in the new and rapidly changing Internet environment.

But *how* distrustful of the attractive offer should we teach people to be? In some cases the answer is easy. Rachel Benner, an Assistant Professor of counseling psychology at the University of Albany, New York, rightly became distrustful in the following scenario. She received an email ostensibly from her Dean saying that he needed help on something important right away. Brenner initially assumed the email was genuine and left her apartment, went to her office, and emailed the Dean that she was ready to meet. When the completely out of character response arrived asking her to buy iTunes gift cards for the Dean's cousin's birthday, she rightly became suspicious and did not take the words at face value.[8] Just as this book is going to press, that particular phish has become an epidemic in higher education and affected one of the coauthors. Coauthor Sloan is a department head for a university computer science department, and a hacker sent that spear phishing email to every professor in his department.

The problem is people *routinely* take the words and actions of others at face value. As Bruce Schneier notes, "Just today, a stranger came to my door claiming he was here to unclog a bathroom drain. I let him into my house without verifying his identity, and not only did he repair the drain, he also took off his shoes so he wouldn't track mud on my floors."[9] The more we replace trust with refusals, verifications, and authentications the more we protect against social engineering, but also the more profoundly we change the currently familiar world of trust-mediated social interaction. The misleading information cases illustrate the extent and seriousness of the problem.

Misleading Information

Social engineering often exploits people's propensity to trust that unverified information others offer is true. The former skip tracer

Frank Ahearn illustrates the point with a (non-Internet) example. He was tracking down someone whom he knew had a personal banker. He waited until the banker was out of the office and the assistant would answer the phone. When she did, he said, "I see I missed my private banker, oh well. I am in the middle of a business meeting, and I wrote several checks, I am concerned one of them may have bounced due to lack of funds. Can you check for me please?"[10] She initially refused, explaining he would need to speak to the banker. Ahearn responded by stressing that he "was in a meeting and the situation was dire … If she did not help me, it was possible my business deal would be negatively affected … she chose the lesser of what appeared to be two evils. "Mr. Money your balance is twenty-four-million dollars."[11] Ahearn then asked, "Which account is that?" and she "read off the account number and the past two months transactions."[12]

When you know that one person in the above conversation is a skip tracer, it is easy to think, "She should have been more cautious and not disclosed the information," and indeed, to combat social engineering, we should replace presumptions of trust with refusals to disclose information and demands for verification and authentication. But think about the enormous number of social and commercial interactions in which we take people's words and actions at face value. You may, for example, have known your auto mechanic for years but really know very little about her beyond the fact that she is an auto mechanic and that her efforts seem to keep your car running as it should. The same is true of a wide range of work associates, retail salespeople we encounters, strangers on the street, news reporters, pharmacists, lawyers, professors, students, and so on—indeed on and on. Do you want to live in a world in which refusals, verifications, and authentications replace the trust that is now pervasive?

One way to address this problem is to minimize the need to educate and train people not to trust. We can do that by improving technical defenses against social engineering.

TECHNICAL DEFENSES TO PHISHING
Reducing Fraudulent Email

A lot of phishing consists of emails that appear to come from somebody the recipient knows, because the phisher has spoofed the "From:" address of the email. There are some technical measures that could reduce the amount of spoofed email that gets delivered.

There are three major technical mechanisms for reducing spoofing. These are all protocols that need to be adopted by organizations that are large senders of email to prevent other senders from pretending to be them. So far, adoption has been halting and partial. The three protocols make for IT alphabet soup. They are Sender Policy Framework (SPF), DomainKeys Identified Mail (DKIM), and Domain Message Authentication Reporting and Conformance (DMARC), which sits on top of SPF and DKIM. Essentially, adoption is slow for two reasons. One is that the protocols are somewhat difficult to understand. The other reason is that the protocols involve a trade-off for legitimate senders, between minimizing the chances that somebody else can spoof them, on the one hand, and maximizing the chances that their own legitimate mail will be delivered on the other hand. Almost everybody prioritizes the successful delivery of their own email. Large email senders are unwilling to see a few percentage points of their legitimate emails go undelivered in return for seeing a moderate reduction in the overall volume of spoofed email.

SPF, the oldest of these frameworks, illustrates the point. Recipients can verify the identity of the sender of an incoming email with, if that sender has set up SPF. SPF *has* been very widely adopted by large senders. However, most senders choose settings where email that doesn't pass the SPF credentials check (which might happen for a variety of reasons, not just spoofing) is de facto labeled as "neutral" or "extra scrutiny before delivery" rather than being labeled "fail/do not deliver." Thus, plenty of spoofed email is still delivered.

SPF works with the "envelope-from" field used exclusively by email systems to authenticate the domain (roughly the part after the @-sign in the email) that the email claims to come from. SPF has no effect on the "From:" name that the recipient sees in their email client when reading the email (the "header-from" field). The same is true for DKIM. The most recent of the three protocols, DMARC, sits on top of one or both of SPF and DKIM, and it does tie the from address end users see to the sending address. However, as of this writing, DMARC adoption is still quite low.

A Reminder: Technical Defenses Elsewhere Will (Often) Help

Organizations should be training their employees not to respond to phishing lures. However, that training is not a panacea. A good training program might result in a significant reduction in the rate at which employees will fall for phishing lures. However, studies of such training programs make it very clear that the rate will *not* drop to zero.[13]

This is yet another reminder of the need for organizations to employ defense in depth, that is, to use many different sorts of defenses. Phishing by itself is almost always one early step of many, many steps in a successful hack. Each of the various defenses we discussed in Chapter 3 would stop some attacks at some point after a successful phish.

SECURITY MIND-SET MORE GENERALLY

On the whole, people tend to trust other people. Thus, all an organization's employees are potentially vulnerable to social engineering attacks like phishing. A large organization's IT staff and their supervisors on up through the CEO need to go beyond simply not being too trusting. They need to have a security mindset. That is, it is their job to always be thinking, "What could go wrong and how might some criminal break in? What can we do to stop that?"

One might get a first clue whether a big company's CEO and board of directors have a security mindset simply by checking whether that company has a C-level Chief Information Security Officer (CISO), and if so, whether the CISO reports to either the CEO or Board of Directors or instead to somebody lower in the organization. A recent survey showed that only about half of the organizations have a CISO, and that of those that do, the CISO reports to a Chief Information or Chief Privacy Officer in 39% of the cases.[14] If a company doesn't have a CISO reporting to the CEO or Board of Directors, then that company probably views computer and network security as just one more cost center for the company.

Security mind-set among the IT staff may well determine whether an organization runs any sort of anti-phishing training. In terms of the CIS Critical Security Controls, this would come under #17, "Implement a Security Awareness and Training Program." But there are other aspects as well.

Large organizations that store a lot of sensitive information should occasionally engage professionals to carry out mock attacks to see how secure they really are. This is called "penetration testing," or "pen testing" for short, and is CIS Critical Security Control #18. Another part of security mindset is restricting information about an organization's network infrastructure and computer security to people inside the organization with a need to know. We know from our discussion of Wyndham in Chapter 1, that nobody in power at Wyndham in 2008 or 2009 had much of a security mind-set, and Wyndham had essentially no defenses in place.

Lack of security mind-set also played a role at multiple points in the Target breach. First, Target had a large amount of internal information about its vendor portal on public-facing web pages, which presumably made things easier for the attackers when they were first planning their attack. Additionally, a big factor in the Target breach was Target's IT staff ignoring multiple warnings from their FireEye intrusion detection system, as well as one warning from Symantec anti-malware software. That is the antithesis of a security mindset. Penetration testing might have revealed that Target's IT staff was not responding appropriately to intrusion alerts.

ENDNOTES

1. Mandiant, M-Trends 2016 FireEye 17, https://www.fireeye.com/current-threats/annual-threat-report/mtrends.html. Mandiant is a cybersecurity firm that is now part of FireEye.
2. Mandiant, "M-Trends 2018," 2018, https://www.fireeye.com/current-threats/annual-threat-report/mtrends.html.
3. J. C. Van Marken, *Industrial Social Organization* (Forgotten Books, 2018).
4. We are roughly following G. A. Akerlof and R. J. Shiller, *Phishing for Phools: The Economics of Manipulation and Deception* (Princeton Oxford: Princeton University Press, 2016), ix.
5. Hewlett-Packard Company, *The Wolf* (HP Studios, 2017), https://www.youtube.com/watch?v=U3QXMMV-Srs&vl=en.
6. Aaron J. Ferguson, "Fostering E-Mail Security Awareness: The West Point Carronade," *EDUCASE Quarterly* 28, no. 1, 2005: 54–57.
7. G. Pate, *Look Left, Look Right, Look Left Again*, Brdbk edition (Greene Bark Press Inc., 2013).
8. L. Ellis, "Phishing Scheme Targets Professors' Desire to Please Their Deans—All for $500 in Gift Cards," *The Chronicle of Higher Education*, January 23, 2019, https://www.chronicle.com/article/Phishing-Scheme-Targets/245535.
9. B. Schneier, *Liars and Outliers: Enabling the Trust That Society Needs to Thrive* (John Wiley & Sons, 2012).
10. F. M. Ahearn, *The Fifteen Minute Skip Tracer: Locate Anyone Anywhere, Using Databases, Social Engineering & Social Media* (Independently published, 2018).
11. Ahearn.
12. Ahearn.
13. D. D. Caputo et al., "Going Spear Phishing: Exploring Embedded Training and Awareness," *IEEE Security & Privacy* 12, no. 1, January 2014: 28–38, https://doi.org/10.1109/MSP.2013.106; Hossein Siadati et al., "Measuring the Effectiveness of Embedded Phishing Exercises," in *10th USENIX Workshop on Cyber Security Experimentation and Test (CSET 17)*, 2017.
14. PricewaterhouseCoopers, "Strengthening Digital Society against Cyber Shocks: Key Findings from the Global State of Information Security Survey 2018," 2018, https://www.pwc.com/us/en/services/consulting/cybersecurity/library/information-security-survey/strengthening-digital-society-against-cyber-shocks.html.

CHAPTER 8

Seeing the Forest

An Overview of Policy Proposals

WE CONCLUDE WITH AN overview of our policy proposals. As we noted in Chapter 1, our goal is to match policies to problems, not to work out the details of the policies proposed. We offer a view of the forest, not a detailed examination of individual trees. We begin with the problem to which those proposals respond.

THE PROBLEM

The problem is that businesses fail to approximate two risk management goals. The *business* risk management goal is to minimize the sum of the cost of the defensive measures and all the expected business losses with those defensive measures. The *consumer* risk management goal is to minimize the sum of the cost of the defensive measures and all the expected consumer losses with those defensive measures. The explanation we proposed of the failure to realize the business risk management goal was corporate culture and—more fundamentally—lack of relevant information about costs of breaches and the probabilities of different types of breaches. Our explanation for the failure to realize the consumer risk management goal was lack of information about costs and probabilities and the fact that consumer losses from a data breach are typically a negative externality for businesses.

SUGGESTED SOLUTIONS

We begin with our solution to the lack of information about costs and probabilities. We proposed mandatory reporting.

Mandatory Reporting

The required report consists of checkboxes and questions about the size, type, and estimated costs of a breach, plus attributes about the organization attacked and its defenses. The aggregated information provides a basis for reasonably accurate estimates of the probability of specific types of security incidents of a specific cost.

Assuming sufficiently rational corporate governance, mandatory reporting would result in an adequate incentive to approximate the business risk management goal. Ensuring an adequate approximation of the consumer risk management goal is more complicated. Mandatory reporting by consumers raises significant privacy issues, so we opted instead for government-initiated or government-funded research which focuses on consumers who consent to provide their information. Even with sufficient information, however, profit-driven businesses will ignore consumer losses that are, for the business, a negative externality. We turned to legal liability to create an incentive for businesses to protect consumers against consumer losses.

The proposals—business mandatory reporting, and voluntary consumer reporting plus liability—do not stand on their own. Our policy proposals include recommendations for the three types of vulnerabilities. The proposals form a mutually supportive whole.

Software Vulnerabilities

Mass market end-user facing software has too many vulnerabilities. The basic reason is that the current consumer demand in software markets is for quick to market, easy-to-use, relatively inexpensive software. Such software tends to be vulnerability-ridden. Our proposal was to change consumer demand by creating a market norm under which consumers demanded adequately secure software. If enough consumers conformed to the norm and thereby demanded more secure, less vulnerability-ridden software, profit-driven businesses would provide it. The changed consumer demand we envision is shaped by knowledge of relevant probabilities and costs in regard to data breaches. In this way, the "consumer demand" approach depends on solving the lack of information problem about costs and probabilities.

Why did we propose this "consumer demand" approach when we proposed legal regulation to address security management vulnerabilities? Because creating a market norm has significant advantages over legal regulation. To begin with, norms typically implement fine-grained, flexible constraints. They can constrain a wide variety of different types of interactions while allowing adjustments for different individual or contextual needs. It is difficult for legal regulation to combine a similarly comprehensive and flexible approach. Further, regulations are typically peppered with unexplained general terms such as "reasonable" and "relevant" (as in "all relevant circumstances") and with references to types of entities and functions ("health organizations" and "health professional"). The terms need the contextually sensitive interpretation that norms provide. Further, relying on legal regulation alone to alter behavior has a significant downside. Even at its best, regulation is costly, and compliance is incomplete. Businesses will comply only if the expected loss from noncompliance is greater than the benefits from noncompliance. Businesses may often reach the opposite conclusion, because, while the cost of litigation can be quite high, the probability of incurring that loss can be very low. To see why, it is helpful to distinguish between winning defendants' costs and losing defendants' costs. Winning defendants' costs include attorney fees, court filing fees, and business losses from negative publicity, all of which a defending company incurs even if it prevails in the litigation.

Losing defendants' costs are the sum of winning defendants' costs plus the statutory fines and compensatory and punitive damages that a business may have to pay if it loses the litigation. The probability of having to incur *any* defendants' costs is the product of the probability of being detected and the probability of litigation if detected. Since that compound probability may be quite small, the expected losses for defending companies in general may be small. Notice also that the expected loss for losing defendants is the product of the amount that they will lose, which may be quite large, together with the product of the compound probability of litigation occurring, already mentioned, with the probability that the defendant loses, and that product may be low. The upshot is that legal liability may be far less effective than we would hope.

Security Management Vulnerabilities

We noted that changing consumer demand will not work for security management vulnerabilities. We proposed the FTC actions for security mismanagement. Its broad investigative powers make this an attractive way to address security mismanagement. However, we noted that this proposal too depends on solving the problem of the lack of information needed to estimate the expected loss avoided for a given company from adopting a type of defense against a type of data breach.

Consumers cannot initiate FTC actions, and relying on FTC actions in the case of security management vulnerabilities may seem to deprive consumers of a way for them to seek redress on their own. They may, however, seek redress through the "reasonable standard" laws proposed in Chapter 4.

Human Vulnerabilities

Hackers exploit the human propensity to trust, so the solution is to make people appropriately less trusting. We cautioned that replacing trust with refusals, verifications, and authentications protects against social engineering but greatly reduces the trust that mediates interactions in a wide range of personal, social, political, and commercial interactions. The Nobel Prize-winning economist Elinor Ostrom emphasizes the point using the example of organizations: "Those of us who work in large organizations—universities, research centers, business firms, government offices—participate in a variety of team efforts. In order to do our own work well, we are dependent on others to do their work creatively, energetically, and predictably, and vice versa."[1] Large organizations are just one example. Trust is pervasive. That is Bruce Schneier's point about the plumber who comes to his door: A "stranger came to my door claiming he was here to unclog a bathroom drain. I let him into my house without verifying his identity."[2]

Reducing human vulnerabilities means educating and training people to be less trusting *in certain situations*. We can also reduce the need to distrust by improving technical defenses.

A CHANGING LANDSCAPE

The rise of MSSPs and the emergence of the Internet of Things are changing the information security landscape. The Internet of Things adds a significant layer of complexity to the traditional Internet. Complexity, as we have noted several times, is the enemy of security. In many cases, the sensible way to meet that enemy may be by outsourcing security to an MSSP. With MSSPs in the picture, the study of defenses against data breaches becomes a study of MSSP defenses *and* a study of contractual allocations of risk and liability.

We conclude with two speculations about the future. The first is that MSSPs may develop into the twenty-first century "shortwave radio." The radio was a focal point of the negligence lawsuit in *T.J. Hooper* we discussed in Chapter 4. The tugboat *T.J. Hooper* sank in a storm off the Atlantic coast. The tug did not have a shortwave radio, a new technology at the time. The captain testified that with the radio he would have received reports of the storm and put in at the Delaware breakwater to ride it out in safety. The court held that the owner of the tug was negligent for not equipping the tug with a shortwave radio. The court's reasoning was that the owner could, and should, have easily calculated that the cost of the relatively inexpensive radio was far less than the expected losses from storms. Courts may well hold the same about MSSPs: namely, that business owners could and should easily see that the relatively low cost of using an MSSP is far less than the expected costs to the business and society of data breaches.

If businesses do increasingly outsource security to MSSPs, then it is likely that a number of MSSPs will compete for business clients. A second speculation is that such market competition among MSSPs will open two new avenues for the legal regulation of information security. One is antitrust law to ensure sufficient competition among MSSPs, and the other is Federal Trade Commission regulation to ensure that MSSPs business practices are neither unfair nor deceptive.

ENDNOTES

1. Elinor Ostrom, *Understanding Institutional Diversity* (Princeton, NJ: Princeton University Press, 2005), 4.
2. Bruce Schneier, *Liars and Outliers: Enabling the Trust That Society Needs to Thrive* (New York: John Wiley & Sons, 2012), 1.

Milton Keynes UK
Ingram Content Group UK Ltd.
UKHW022358061024
449327UK00031B/2562